AF328509

Bonheur de Vivre

An overarching quality of Frenchness ran through the 20th century's art, beginning with the Gallic sensibility of the great Henri Matisse, soon to be followed by the Iberian Joan Miró, surely an honorary Frenchman, to the adorably fun-loving American Alexander Calder, who went to Paris as soon as it was possible and soon befriended Miró and later Marcel Duchamp, to evolve into a Frenchman like a caterpillar to a butterfly. It was Duchamp who gave the name Mobile to what Calder was creating, where you can see the red circular form in the Miró turn up in the flat parts of the three-dimensional mobile, light as a feather blowing in a gentle wind, a gasp of air, to find itself mirrored in his fellow American Robert Motherwell's paper collages, which he had originally made at the suggestion of the Francophile Peggy Guggenheim and who had already discovered the wonder in all things in the forties collage which he titled Joy of Living and who said that seeing his first Matisse shot him to his heart like an arrow. And then along came another Californian, Sam Francis, who as soon as he could also moved to Paris and soon enough made his own French art and during his years in the City of Light the first painting he sold was to Madame Matisse!. He would much later seek me out to work with him and I loved his work for its sheer beauty and for its sense of light and life and joy and the absolute happiness that emanated from those white canvases and white, white sheets of paper that recalled so much the Frenchness of Matisse. When we first started to work together he said 'Let's have some fun!', and that's exactly what we did. When I stayed with him in Santa Monica, his bookshelves filled with many books of French philosophy and so many books by and on Matisse, I'd sleep soundly there, with a Miró print above my head. When I met Calder in the sixties he was now back in America but the work remained "French" and when I met Motherwell he was by now an American giant, although so Gallic, he came into the small gallery I worked in on 57th Street, to get a collage made from a French bleu Gauloises pack framed as a gift for the Maitre d'Hotel of the Four Seasons. Can there be anything more French than that?

And so the twentieth century had begun, virtually at its dawning, with Matisse, had passed through Miró soon afterwards, later to be taken up by the American Frenchness of Calder and Motherwell and ending with the shimmeringly French paintings of Sam Francis. It was as if the American Century was actually the French Century, as it had already been throughout the nineteenth century.

But the story need not end there. The Yorkshireman, William Tillyer, of Huguenot origin, came into my life in 1970 and we have worked together ever since. His art, so inspired by American culture, is actually French in feeling and it honours the qualities of the French and American French art, brimming over with Love, Joy, Colour, Passion, Light, Fun, Beauty, those very words that seem from a distant and foreign country and from a long, long, time ago. Sam Francis loved his work and bought a watercolour.

Bernard Jacobson, December 2015

The Necessity of Beauty

Mel Gooding

'Beauty is truth; truth beauty, – that is all
Ye know on earth, and all ye need to know.'
John Keats 'Ode on a Grecian Urn'

'Sensation, revelation.' Georges Braque (*Cahiers*)

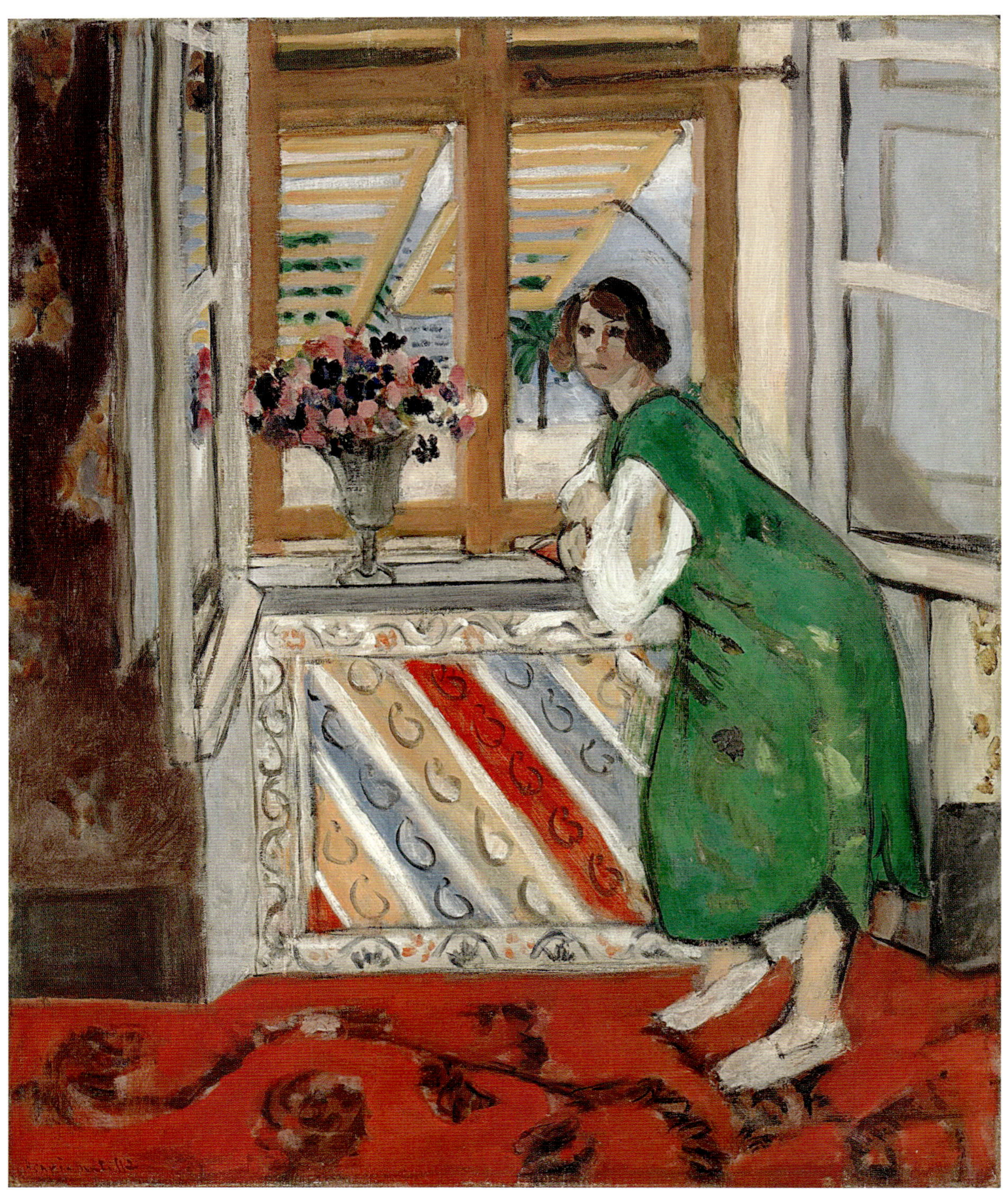

Henri Matisse (1869-1954)
Jeune fille à la mauresque, robe verte
1921
Oil on canvas
66 x 55 cm (26 x 21⅝ ins)

I Material Presence: The Simultaneity of Art

'The business of art is to reveal the relation between man and his circumambient universe at the living moment.' (D. H. Lawrence)

Henri Matisse: *Jeune Fille à la Mauresque. Robe verte* (1921)

A young woman awkwardly leans on the windowsill, in Nice in 1921; the window and its shutters, both interior and exterior, are wide open: the world has entered the room; its warm air carries into the interior the scent of a vase crammed with sweet peas. Dressed in a shapeless green shift over a loose sleeved silk blouse, she turns to look back, into the space of the room, at the artist, whose place we have taken. In this way implicated in the dialectical to-and-fro of spectatorship, the reflective mirror-play of painting, we look back at her, and beyond: our gaze penetrates aerial space, beyond palm trees and the sunlit *plage* to a pale blue morning sea.

In a radio broadcast of 1942, asked where the charm of his pictures of open windows comes from, Matisse replied: 'probably from the fact that for me the space is one unity from the horizon right to the interior of my work room, and that the boat that is going exists in the same space as the familiar objects around me; and the wall with the window does not create two different worlds.' This is to describe in the most vivid way, Gaston Bachelard's 'intimate immensity'. 'Immensity', writes Bachelard, 'is a philosophical category of reverie.' The reverie of 'contemplation produces an attitude that is so special, an inner state that is so unlike any other, that the daydream transports the dreamer outside the immediate world to a world that bears the mark of infinity.'

We are present in that one unified, sweet-scented space in marine light; we share it with the woman in green. But the painting is *here*: it is a material object in our present space. It has its own, distinctive, unique, objective dynamics: form, light and colour. Above all '… light plays the leading role', says Matisse, 'colour comes second; it's with colour that you put down light, of course, but above all you must feel this light, have it within yourself.' That sharp implacable green! The pale blues, reds, purples! We remark at once the tactile strokes of a variably loaded brush; and the rhythmic, vertical interplay of the orthogonal – the window frame and shutters, subtly various in perspective, in relation to our

viewpoint, – the wall's diagonals, blue, ochre, red, and the arabesques in the dense red carpet. It is not there, in 1921, looking out to the *Baie des Anges*, that we find ourselves: rapt, we are playing a beautiful game, in the here and now, in our immediate and present time and space, in front of this radiant object.

I intend the title of this essay. It is, of course, a stronger restatement of the title of Hans-Georg Gadamer's seminal 1961 essay, 'The Relevance of the Beautiful', in which the great aesthetician considered the meaning of art under three heads, assimilating the creative impulse, as experienced by both maker and receiver, to the essentially anthropological categories of play, symbol and festival. Notwithstanding my admiration for Gadamer's essay, I will make my own use, and my own elaborations, of those headings, which seem to offer illumination of a common aesthetic dynamics that underlies the particular and distinctive power and beauty of the otherwise disparate work of each of the five artists featured in this remarkable exhibition. It is an exhibition that is itself presented in the celebratory spirit and largesse that is definitive of 'festival'.

There are two common assumptions that recur in much of the contemporary discourse around visual art, and which seem to make uncomfortable those who would want to assert the humanistic value and power of art as an enhancement of ordinary, everyday life, a vital agency in the intensifying of our 'examination' of it, and of our sense of its fullness. With regard to the former, I have in mind Socrates: 'The unexamined life is not worth living.' And to the latter, I think of Susan Sontag: 'What is beautiful reminds us of nature as such – and of what lies beyond the human and the made – and thereby stimulates and deepens our sense of the sheer spread and fullness of reality, inanimate as well as pulsing, that surrounds us all.' I claim that it is precisely that sense of the beautiful, as opposed what is merely 'interesting', that is central to our experience of much art, and is indeed deeply 'relevant' to our current needs; and that the art of the past, as we experience it, is always dynamically present, always contemporaneous.

The first of those common assumptions is that the word 'beauty' has no place in the discourse, being a quality without a definition, an empty word, a meaningless, 'merely subjective' assertion of value. It is permitted, of course, as a problematic term within the history of philosophical aesthetics. Beyond that, it is merely an indicator of snobbish or elitist connoisseurship, the exercise of 'good taste', whether it is institutionally sanctioned, by the museum or the high-class dealer or saleroom, or hierarchically validated, by 'curators' or 'experts'. 'Taste' is essentially unarguable: a connoisseur is, by definition, 'one who knows"; the term itself is exclusive of those who don't. It is the case, however, that there are many outside those elites who frequently use the term 'beautiful' as an emphatic description of that which in some ways moves them: these will argue that its use may be merely subjective, but that its history gives it a special resonance, a particular effect.

The second assumption is that art as a social phenomenon has changed, as it always has in the last century and a half, and that what demands our attention now is an art of 'interesting' and purposively thought-provoking, critical or controversial engagement with societal issues and economic and socio-political relations. The art of our time is, it is said, is 'performative', an art of actions, transactional or 'relational' situations and environments, or it is an art of ambiguous – sometimes simply blank – objects and ironic tableaux. This is an art to which the consumer should not look for solace or comfort, expecting, rather, to suffer anxious disturbance, emotional and intellectual ambiguity and existential anguish, or, in the face of reflectively ironic spectacle, simply to enjoy a cynical laugh.

A great deal of the art work, in any media, that might be subsumed under these descriptions claims for itself creative-critical, and moral, authority as enacting necessary truths in the face of inauthenticity, the bad faith of bourgeois life under late global capitalism. Such art is, however, avidly collected by those who have made their wealth out of such a life, and are seemingly untouched by such inconvenient truths or untroubled by the anxieties they might be supposed to induce. These fortunates also enjoy the satisfaction of knowing that as collectors they have special access to the company of the 'art world' cognoscenti of commercially successful artists, museum curators, gallerists and dealers. The cognoscenti are, by definition, 'those in the know'; the term excludes those who are not. The irony in this world is not confined to the art.

Certainly, what *not* to seek in much of contemporary art is the quality in things that were once described as 'beautiful': among other things, harmony of colour and form, the vision of colour and light, the inspiriting dynamics of formal relations – geometric or otherwise, the quasi pleasures of rhythm and interval, the joys of intellect and intuition, transformative artistic control in the face of chaos, and the evocation of what we find 'beautiful' – without embarrassment – in nature. In short, those things which bring, as Sontag reminds us with the most eloquent simplicity, 'what ordinary language extols as beautiful – a gladness to the senses.'

To find that 'gladness' requires us to look beyond much contemporary art, and to approach again the best of 20th century art, not as curiously historical – 'Art is over' –, or as *examples* of particular movements or *isms*, or as evidence of one phase or another of an out-dated historicist account of 'modern art', but, rather, as immediate to our experience in the living moment of the here-and-now. We should acknowledge, indeed, that all art is simultaneous, happening in the instant of our encounter with it. Trapped, as we are, within the temporal reality of a life, and with only one way out, the art we encounter, wherever – in Egypt, Florence, Amsterdam, London, Berlin, etc. – and whenever, exists in our time and space at the moment; is at once objectively – i.e. materially – *present*, in both senses: ineluctably so. The study of History, in whatever form, may bring further dimensions to these present, or to later, encounters, as it might properly be regarded as an important aspect of the discourse that brings meanings to those encounters. But it has no privilege in that discourse, for the meanings of which I speak must be made out of all the things that occur to us, and of anything that impinges upon our being and knowing, and that complex experience can belong only to us, each in our given condition.

This is what Gadamer means by 'the relevance' of the beautiful: that which pertains to – is *pertinent* to – our reality, created out of the discourse, which is the shared definition of meanings and the common pursuit of judgments, however provisional both may be, in which we engage with others. It cannot exist in isolation; we have no such 'reality' without the dialogical intercourse that creates the variegated structures of shared meanings. There must be an object for such creative exchange: art is one of those objects. The great early theorists of dialogic criticism, Mikhail Bakhtin and Pavel Medvedev, put this clearly: 'All the products of ideological creation – works of art, scientific works, religious symbols and rites, etc. – are material things, part of a practical reality that surrounds man. It is true that these are things of a special nature, having significance, meaning, inner value. But these meanings and values are embodied in material things and actions. They cannot be developed outside of some developed material.'

This is the 'necessity' of my title. A sense of beauty – Sontag's 'sense of the sheer spread and fullness of reality, inanimate as well as pulsing, that surrounds us,' and the 'gladness of the senses' it brings with it, is a precondition of a certain kind of discovery, or invention, of meanings and truths. Always, as I have said, necessarily provisional, open to further development and change. The work of art addresses the mind through the senses, through effect, that is the meaning of *aesthesis*: sensation, perception. The mind responds in its constructive critical contribution – combining the cognitive and the affective, thought and feeling – to the unending discourse. That is how art works.

As opposed to the *effect* of painting, and collage, and sculpture, which combines precise sensations and more or less vague thought, *meaning* in painting etc. is discovered in critical negotiations that must be conducted in natural language, and which have as their end shared feelings, understandings and judgments. 'A painting has to exude more than an effect', wrote Mark Tobey, the American painter. '"Man's true world is his thought and his thought is reflected in his art as well as in everything else he does.' Conversation, critical and otherwise, is a large part of everything else he does. And its centrality to human realisation must have ethical implications. It is a good. Wittgenstein stated this with extreme economy: 'Ethics and aesthetics are one.'

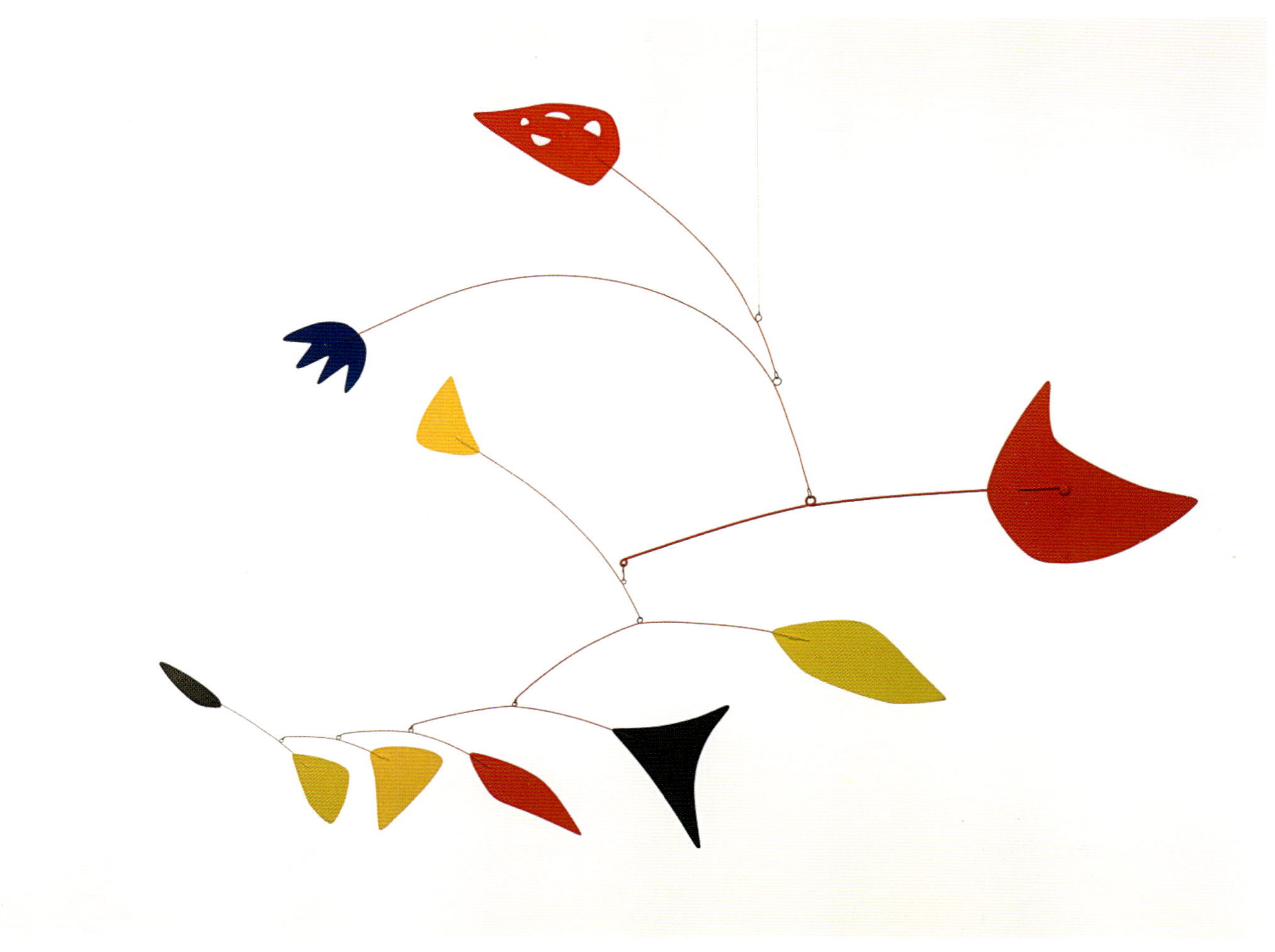

Alexander Calder (1898-1976)
Blue Flower, Perforated Red
1960
Hanging mobile: painted sheet metal and wire
165.1 x 127 x 121.9 cm (65 x 50 x 48 in)

II Art as Play: The Joy of Living

'The first thing we must make clear to ourselves is that play is so elementary a function of human life that culture is inconceivable without it.' (Hans-George Gadamer)

Alexander Calder: *Blue Flower, Perforated Red* (1960)

These momentous silhouettes – one of them a blue flower, the others vague shapes of things organic, leaves perhaps – one perforated, as if touched by autumn's ravage – , petals or buds, a fish's tail, a bird glimpsed in flight, hover, swing, maintain a momentary miraculous poise, a beautiful tremulous configuration, never to be seen again, as things in nature are to be seen never again as they are at a moment of stillness. A momentary stillness is a phase in the *perpetuum mobile* of the natural world. Not a metaphor, this hanging mobile of gaily painted sheet metal and wire: it is a thing in its own aerial *thinginess*, which like other things perceived in a moment will remind us, irresistibly, of something else, somewhere else, some time else.

And this delicate mechanism, as it moves, plays an endless game of changing relations, the spaces between its shapes and the vacancies between its lovely, branching, curving lines always and ever different, unprecedented. The artist masterminds this playful movement, just as, as a young man in Paris, he was the comically insouciant, creative ringmaster of his magical, always provisional, *cirque Calder*. Who had ever thought of setting such a thing in perpetual motion? It was in Piet Mondrian's studio in 1930 that this most brilliant and original of ideas came to Calder's playful mind: why not set Mondrian's coloured squares in motion? And why stop at the rectangular? He realised at once that he had found his own way to abstraction.

Colour, shape and design are aspects of abstraction, indicators of resemblance. It was Wallace Stevens, the American poet, who spoke of the 'resemblance between things as one of the significant components of the structure of reality.' All art is the revelation of resemblances. Abstraction uncovers, and brings into play, hidden aspects of that 'structure' of which Stevens spoke. "What interests me in all paintings' said Alberto Giacometti, 'is resemblance – that is, what is resemblance for me: something that makes me discover more of the world.'

The key to play as an idea in aesthetics, and in art, is that it is an aspect of the experience of art that is common to artist and spectators alike, albeit different in ways specific to their roles and their histories. As with any spectator sport, or drama, or any other form of spectacle, such as the circus, the game is played, so to speak, by all present at the event. Looking at paintings etc. is indubitably a happening, in time and space. So we may properly speak of both the maker's and the spectator's enjoyment of art as a form of play: in each case it is disinterested and without what we would normally think of as utility; and it constitutes a time out of time, special not ordinary. Within the closed circle of the game, both artist and spectator as players are, of course, governed by powerfully purposive impulses; they must act within given rules of engagement. We also speak, sensibly, of the 'uses of art', but what we really mean by that is its *usefulness* in an aspect of our lives that is itself beyond immediate practicality but nevertheless desirable.

The effect of art, in this light, is analogous to the erotic: Erotic pleasurableness may encourage and enhance procreation, but is not necessary to it. The aesthetic like the erotic, is sufficient as an end in itself: pleasure, *jouissance* (notwithstanding the fun and complication of Roland Barthes's play with the word) bliss, gladness. Art offers the artist, like the footballer or the gymnast, the pleasure of direct involvement in the movement and transformation of materials and circumstances; it offers the spectator the joy of imaginative engagement with what cannot be ordered and shaped by will. We may participate in the game, as player or spectator, without any certainty of its outcome, and with the enjoyable tension that that brings in anticipation of a pleasurable resolution. No one knows how a game will end and no one knows when an artwork has exhausted its possibilities of meaning.

Follow the movement of a Calder mobile; examine the strangely transformed piece of arbitrarily folded packing paper in a Motherwell collage; look into the space of a Matisse room, enveloped by its patterned wallpaper; let the mind ponder the oddly moving relation between Miró's linear figures, birds, humans, heavenly bodies, against an stained and abraded sky; contemplate the spontaneous, momentary actions recorded in the scattered colours across the surfaces of a Sam Francis painting: as in the unpredictable moments of a game, these are experiences beyond thought, apprehensions that do not admit of any fixed comprehensions. Interpretative participation, at first immediate and unspoken, then considered and articulated, is all.

The act of painting, or the making of a collage or a mobile, however primitive or sophisticated its technology, and whatever the technical resources of the artist, has complex determinations. Among many others, these may include: the primary impulse to create, which in the case of great artists such as those in this exhibition, this will amount to an ineluctable passion; a sophisticated awareness of a potential audience; an awareness, more or less profound, of the work of other artists, past and present, and a sense of being in a creative, and critically relation to what those other artists have made; a heightened, i.e. trained and developed, sense of the world, of its diversity and heterogeneity. Different painters bring different experiences, different temperaments, different intentions, different talents, etc. to their work: no two artists are equipped or motivated to act in the same way. And that is true also of the spectators of the work.

Notwithstanding the non-purposive nature of art, or even the compulsive actions that often create both art and artist, every artist may be said *to intend* the work he or she makes. Its intended function is to provoke the free play of discourse that will discover the range and depth of its possible shared meanings, and that will give it critical, and thereafter, historical, validity. Its greatness within the discourse cannot be determined by any intrinsic value. What could that possibly be? the work of art is a physical, not a metaphysical, object. It will be determined by 'posterity', as Duchamp observed in a short text in 1956, which concurs, succinctly, with Gadamer's aesthetics: 'All in all, the creative act is not performed by the artist alone; the spectator brings the work in contact with the external world by deciphering and interpreting its inner qualifications and so adds his contribution to the creative act. This becomes even more obvious when posterity gives its final verdict and sometimes rehabilitates forgotten artists.'

Artists conduct their search for a new reality, and the work that will in some way embody and communicate it, through an imaginative and largely intuitive, purely playful engagement with the actualities of the world, and within established conventions that they constantly renew or break, as they extend or change the rules of engagement. 'The painter takes his body with him' said Paul Valéry. Merleau-Ponty added: '[Indeed], we cannot imagine how a *mind* could paint…. It is by lending his body to the world that the artist changes the world into paintings. To understand these transubstantiations we must go back to the working, actual body – not the body as a chunk of space or a bundle of functions but that body which is an intertwining of vision and movement.' That last phrase could as well describe the bodily action of a great sportsman, a Federer, a Messi, a Muhammad Ali, players whom we do not hesitate to call artists, and whose work we readily describe as beautiful.

Movement and artistic gesture are transformative; the body acts upon the materials provided: the placing, and gluing down, of one fragment of paper on another; the action of the painter's arm as it describes a zigzag or an arabesque; the rubbing of a pastel stick across a stained ground to create a halo of light; the splash of thinned acrylic on to the canvas; the flick of a finger that sets a thin metal shape at the end of a wire into a quiver or a floating action through thin air. In the immediate presence of the living work we imaginatively enter in the game; we re-enact the action, transforming it into subjective experience, we possess the work, we take it into ourselves. We are surprised by joy.

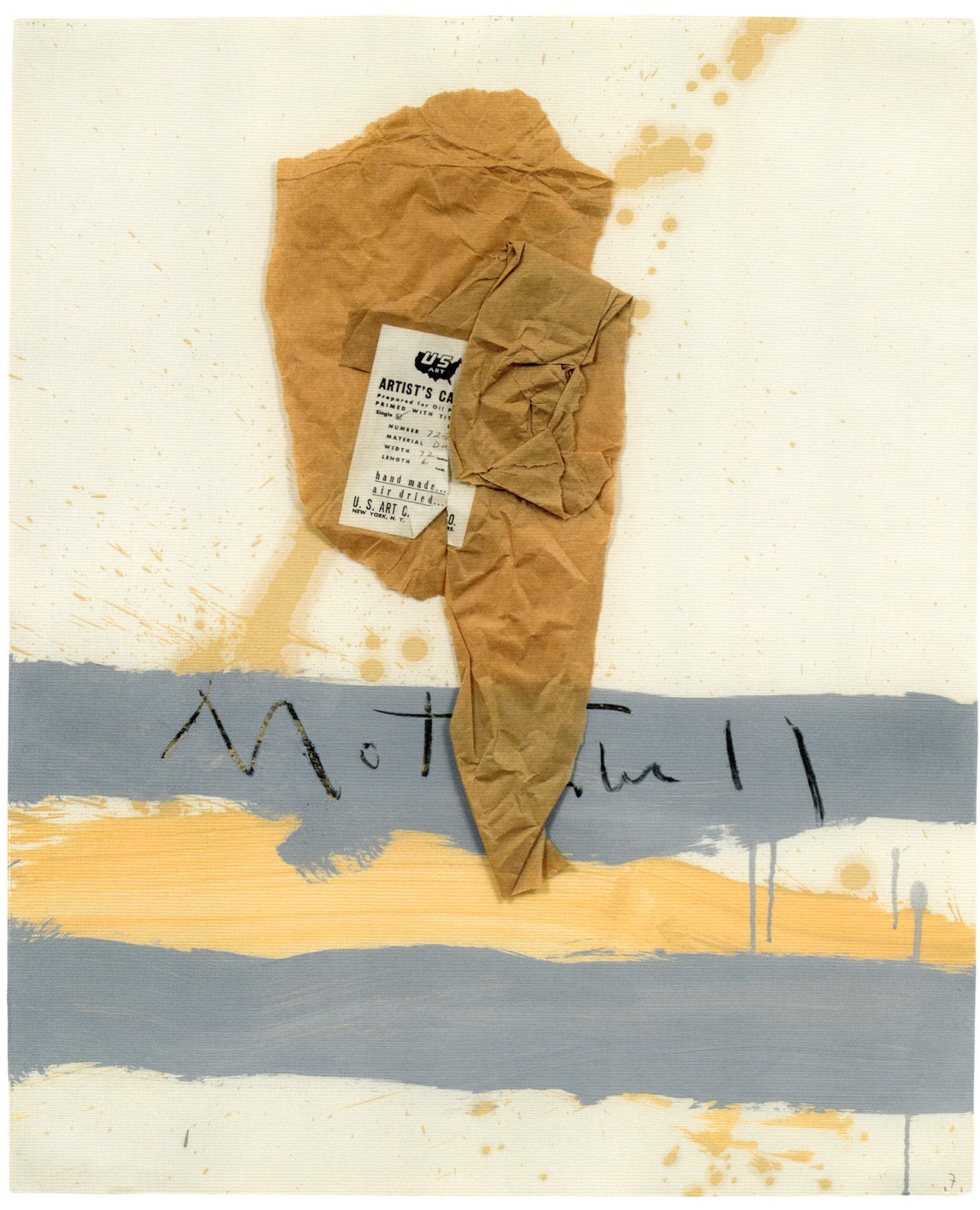

Robert Motherwell (1915-1991)
U.S. Art New York N.Y.
1962
Oil and pasted paper on paper
73.7 x 58.4 cms (29 x 23 ins)

III Art as Symbol: Coherence in the Work of Art

'*Pulcra sunt quae visa placent.*' ('That is beautiful the apprehension of which pleases.')
(Thomas Aquinas)

Robert Motherwell: *U.S Art New York N.Y* (1962)

Two roughly parallel ragged bars of pale blue – *sea-blue* – oil paint, each laid in one expressive lateral stroke on to a similarly summary stroke of pale ochre – sand-colour: a common enough, even childlike, sign for a tidal sea and sand view – one wave after another, rolling inshore. On the upper blue bar-stroke is the artist's signature, boldly figured in black oil stick with enough emphatic pressure to become an inscription: *Motherwell.* Rising with the ungovernable ejaculatory energy of a splatter, a sea spray of thinned ochre, with a light aureole of oil stain, splashes up and over the top edge of the paper support.

Imposed upon this evocation of seaside, and, by implication, sexual happiness – *bonheur de vivre* – is the collage element of folded and scrunched brown packing paper, whose label gives the work its deadpan title. Both as a physical fact and a symbolic image, this intervention is a starkly banal, arbitrary, and somewhat comic, reminder of the world of quotidian consciousness, to which we must return after luxurious reverie and sensuous pleasure: it starkly compromises the vital celebration of creative *jouissance* manifest in both the image itself and in the procedures of its energetic production. It functions as a mildly minatory commentary on the theme of *volupt*é, of rapt excess: it resembles, among other things, a kind of ironic thumbs down.

These oppositions and contradictions, and there are others implicit, are held together, coherently *contained* in a singularly ambiguous object-image. Like certain others of the New York School, Motherwell, steeped in Surrealism, and devoted to automatism as a creative principle, did not shy from the symbol in either of its possible manifestations: as a motif with possible meanings (ambiguous or otherwise) or implications; or as the totality of meaning carried by the work as a whole. Motherwell's playfulness also had a Surrealist validation: "I took to collage like a duck to water,' he wrote; and, as he put it, he 'played with papers' throughout his artistic life. The title of a collage he made in 1948, *The Best Toys are Made of Paper*, derived from a poem written by his friend the writer-critic Harold Rosenberg for his daughter, a poem that is like a little collage itself:

The best toys are paper that opens in surprise
Or a lost umbrella dancing on its one leg
Stars on strings of infancy.

————————————

Making art is, ultimately, a philosophical activity, albeit of a special kind, having its own characteristic modes of representation, which are visual, and which are not those of natural language. Whenever we speak of 'the language of painting' – or of collage, etc. – we are employing a metaphor; just as we are, in reverse, when we say 'I see what you mean', or 'look at it this way'. By 'philosophical' I mean, in the broadest sense, that it is concerned with the discovery of meaning in the welter of the world, the pursuit of a version of truth, the definition of a portion of reality. ('Philosophy' defines itself as 'love of truth'.) Art doesn't work at all like natural language, though a work of visual art is, in itself, indeed something analogous to a Wittgenstein 'language game', enigmatically propositional. Visual art transforms the world not by translating it into the abstract codes of speech and writing, but by entering real space and time as an object with particular properties.

How does art 'transform the world'? To begin with, it presents us with material objects in which the processes of a magic transformation remain visible and palpable. Looking at a work, we encounter matter transformed and energised. The artist does not express himself, as in discursive speech and writing: it is *the work* that is expressive. It is the work that reflects the world and discovers and reveals meaning to the apprehending subject – the spectator who engages with the work. The 'world' of which I speak comprehends all the inner worlds that we contain within our experience of 'being-in-the-world'. Artists are concerned with the revelation of reality, which entails the transformation of matter into symbol. This transformation is something that happens through the painter's action on specific materials using particular technologies: beating and painting sheet metal, 'playing with papers', drawing, painting or splattering pigmented matter on to a support.

The outcome is an object having expressive force, what the great American aesthetician Suzanne Langer calls 'vital import': that 'element of *felt life* objectified into the work, made amenable to our understanding. In this way, and in no other essential way, a work of art is a symbol.' Those memorable phrases 'vital import' and 'felt life', catch at the quick of art, point to its vibrancy: the vibrancy that animates Matisse's and Miró's paintings, that is enacted in the tremulous mobile, that is expressed in Francis's splash and splatter, his gestures in white space, and that is realised in Motherwell's manipulations of paint and paper. Heidegger more than once reminds us that the Greek word *techne* from which we derive *technique, technology*, etc. and which relates to the concept of *art* (skill at making) and the creating of *artefacts* (things made with technical skill), originally meant 'a letting something appear, which brings something made, as something present, among things that are already present.' Art, the skill of the artist, is at the service of the energies that release matter into form; and the unconscious plays its part in that mysterious transaction between the painter and the materials of the art, as do the unpredictable factors of accident and physical process.

We may acknowledge these artists as makers of instructive and beautiful *representations* – figurative or otherwise – of the seen and felt world; and yet how different they are from each other, and from other artists. It cannot be that what is seen and felt changes: the sky and sea are always blue, human features are, more or less, constant, but always different, the moon and stars appear in every night sky, leaves caught in a slight breeze, quiver. The differences must consist in the way in which the given world is apprehended, in the manner of its visualisation, in its infinite artistic *realisations*. This is not merely a matter of style: it is a matter of *vision*, in its primary as well as in its metaphorical sense, and of imagination. The imagination is the shaping faculty that assimilates the visual and the sensible world to mental and psychological reality. The imaginative vision of the artist seizes upon the sensuous facts that the world presents, Rilke's 'dear visible and tangible', and transforms them into *symbolic* re-presentations.

When we look at a painting we enter into a dynamic relation with a symbolic object: we construct, in a kind of collaboration with the artist, a reality from the actual. The *actual* is what exists, whether we know of its existence or not; the *real* is what we make of what exists, as we encounter it, in the act of recognition, which is the knowing of something in such a way that we may know it again. The artist is not so much concerned with the world as it actually exists, as with the world as something to be *transformed*, to be re-invented, or to be re-constructed. This act of transformation, or invention, or construction, call it what you will, is informed by truth. The aesthetic action becomes an ethical action. This is what Heidegger meant when he said that art was 'the setting-into-work of truth' and that art 'lets truths originate.' That is to say: every painting is the beginning of new possibilities of reality.

In our contemplation of the art-work, the 'gladness' we may feel, as we know, will have something to do with our sense of it as a composed thing. The importance of this aspect, to what is sometimes called 'composition', by which we mean the ways in which the parts compose themselves into the whole, is not to be underestimated. For Matisse it was a paramount consideration: 'Composition is the art of arranging in a decorative manner the diverse elements at a painter's command to express his feelings. In a picture every part will be visible and will play its appointed role, whether it be principal or secondary… A work of art must be harmonious in its entirety; any superfluous detail would replace some other essential detail in the mind of the spectator.'

We note that Matisse moves seamlessly from the making of an image to the reception of it. He writes as the maker and of his feelings, but he knows, as do we, that in the reception of the work, it is not the artist's feelings that matter, but those of the spectator. That reversal of roles is at the heart of the symbolic transaction occasioned by the work. We know that Matisse, and I would assume that it is a dream shared by every great artist, at certain moments in their creative lives, dreamed of 'an art of balance, of purity and serenity, devoid of troubling or depressing subject matter, an art that could be for every mental worker, for the businessman as well as the man of letters, for example, a soothing, calming influence on the mind…' If this somewhat surprisingly associates the complacent desires of the bourgeois collector and gallery goer with the residue of Aquinian aesthetics, then that is because Matisse was both a transcendent artist and a man of the world.

Here is Stephen Dedalus: 'To finish what I was saying about beauty, said Stephen, the most satisfying relations of the sensible must therefore correspond to the necessary phases of artistic apprehension. Find these and you will find the qualities of universal beauty. Aquinas says: *Ad pulcritudinem tria requiruntur integritas, consonantia, claritas.* I translate it so: *Three things are needed for beauty, wholeness, harmony and radiance.*' (*A Portrait of the Artist as a Young Man*) Joyce, like Stephen, was well aware that Aquinas's aesthetics were an aspect of his theology. But these formulations of the great Thomas may resonate in the discourse of a purely secular aesthetics. For his 'three things' may be seen as the 'balance, purity and serenity' of Matisse's definition of composition. And behind this lies the deeper thought.

If a work of art, whether it is a painting, a collage, a mobile or a sculpture, is composed with the kind of rigour demanded by Matisse, then it behoves us to pay attention to that aspect of its being. Miró described it in another way: 'I try to apply colors like words that shape poems, like notes that shape music.' As a poem and music are, by definition, composed, we must read and listen with heightened attention in order to compose it again, for ourselves, as readers, as listeners. So in our encounter with the visual work of art we must make it again, we must ourselves re-make the work. Miró speaks of 'a physical sensation to begin with, followed up by an impact on the psyche.' Criticism is a composed articulation of that 'impact', the utterance of a heightened kind of attention and response.

Let us come back to the spectator in front of the work. The object of contemplation, the totality of the work, image and support, the material embodiment of the artistic intention, whatever that may be, is that which Langer calls the 'art symbol' or the 'expressive form.' This symbolic object has diverse parts, and these may include form and image, material colour, representational and abstract elements, and specifically symbolic motifs, colours, and forms, depending on the subject or purpose of the work. The composition will will constitute the articulation of the parts into a whole, harmonious or not. To these practical features we will give the full conscious attention that is the beginning of criticism and interpretation.

But Miró's reference to the 'psyche' hints at more. Uniting the object and its parts there exists a cohesion compounded of object and image, material and sign, idea and realisation. It is what might be called the symbolic coherence of the work. It is in the apprehension of this coherence that we find the beauty of the work: an apprehension – a taking hold of – that comprehends the workings of intellect and emotion, the combination of thought and feeling, the interaction of mind and matter, the phenomenological immediacy of space and time, and a pleasure of the senses that is indistinguishable from the discernment of meaning. Beauty defined in this way is material and phenomenological: it cannot exist without an object, without the experiencing subject, and without the discourse that brings meaning. This beauty is culturally embedded and may be shared; it is a vital component of the reality of a work of art. The real is a coherence we create with others: it is a beautiful construction.

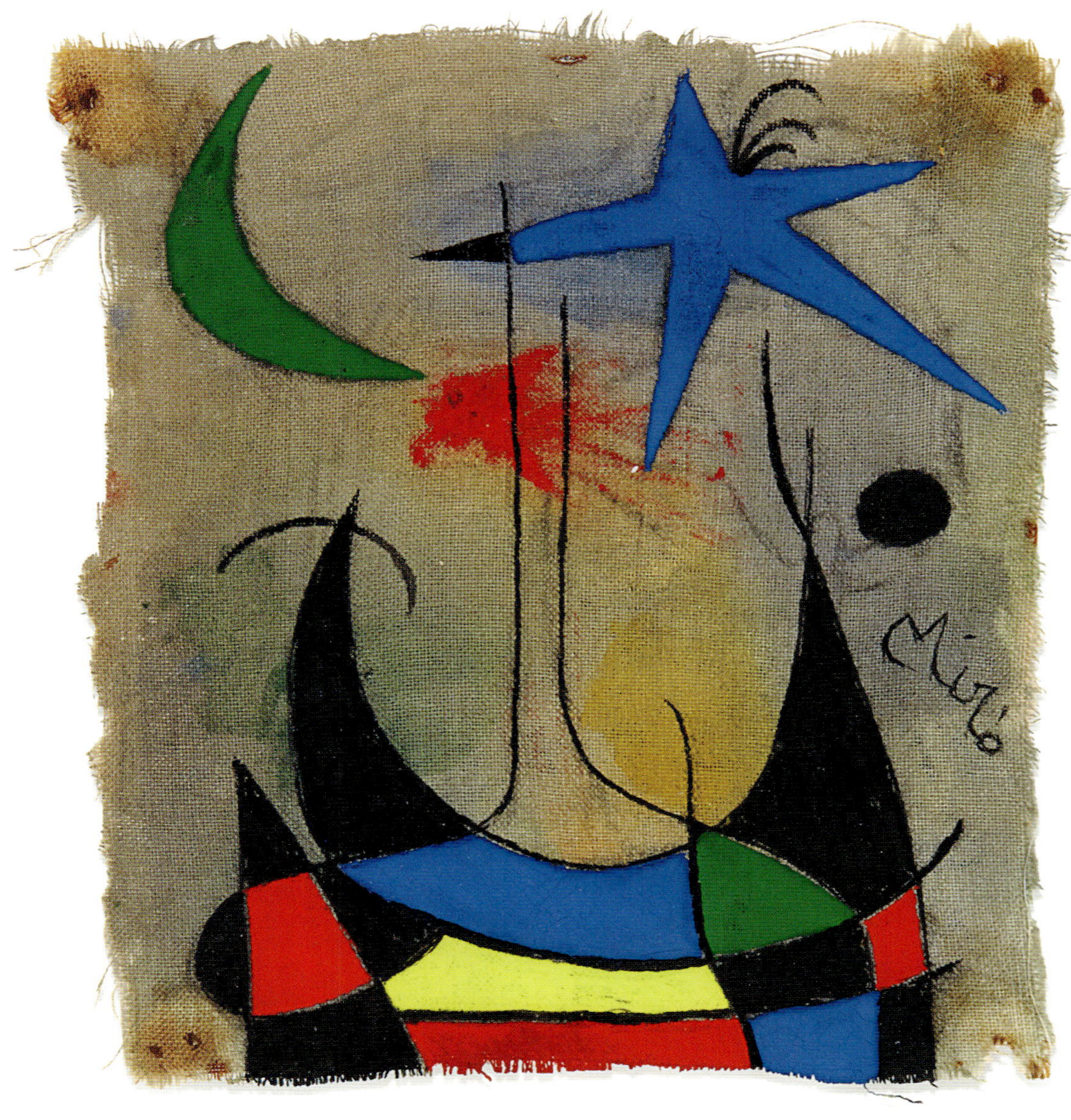

Joan Miró (1893-1983)
Femme amoureuse de l'étoile filante
1966
Oil on Canvas
13 x 12 cms (5⅛ x 4¾ ins)

IV Festival: The Polyphony of Creative Criticism

What we create: is it ours? (André Breton)

Joan Miró: *Femme amoureuse de l'étoile filante* (1966)

We live in a miraculous universe. Its cold indifference, its immeasurable magnitude, its deathly actuality, its indescribable beauty: all meaningless. As Guy Davenport has observed, it is, however, coherent: 'the universe is harmonic, or it wouldn't work.' Notwithstanding that, the universe is not a work of art. You cannot *interpret* the universe, or make a judgment of it. Art transforms it, makes it ours. Look at this shooting star and this green moon, this black planet and this scarlet fire-burst in the evening sky! Miró made this work; his signature, which is written, unabashed, in that self-same sky, proclaims it. But from wherever it came from, this image-object, its heavenly bodies painted on to a tiny piece of frayed and ragged canvas, it is now indubitably ours, it has fallen into our space like the star it portrays; it burns with energy.

Star, moon and planet are not the only heavenly bodies in this image: there is that of the woman who has fallen in love with the star, who reaches up to embrace its falling figure, whose every nerve and sinew extends to entrap and hold it, draw it into her body. What ecstasy we anticipate, what beautiful resolution and consummation of this desire of the earthly for the heavenly. The rejoicing extends to the protagonists and the cosmic spectators of this triumph of love: the moon and the dark planet are held in poise as if components of a Calder mobile; the woman in love is arrayed in festive colours; the firework bursts in a sky lit by the rays of the declining sun, an unearthly halo of gold for the earthly female. We are long way from Nice in 1921, but as with the ravishing Matisse, as we look into this tiny work, we experience 'a physical sensation… followed up by an impact on the psyche.' An excitement of eye and mind merge in our contemplation. One work, in this context, reminds us of another that shares the same festive space. The eye darts from one to another, as does the mind. And a reverie of love cannot but accompany our complex delight in both paintings.

———————————

'A festival' writes Gadamer, is 'an experience of community and represents community in its most perfect form. A festival is meant for everyone.' The celebratory occasion of festival, seen in this light of shared, communal experience, may serve as an appropriately positive metaphor for a central desideratum of aesthetic experience, the recognition of critical discourse as a shared celebration of art, essential to the search for meaning, coherence and beauty in art. The individual encounter with art is always, in some ways or others, preceded by elements of the discourse, for we approach art through a drizzle of words, in a culture saturated by natural language. We take to it personal memories and cultural recollections: we have talked before, we sometimes talk through, and we talk after, the encounter. And our efforts to bring into focus the symbolic coherence of a work i.e. to experience its beauty – that which is many ways *beyond* language – may be enhanced by our attempts, however faltering and banal, to discuss the work in any of its aspects.

Natural phenomena also engender a celebratory discourse, as waterfalls and sunsets provoke the faculty of wonder, the experience of a beauty that nobody disputes as controversial or meaningless. But it does not involve the consideration of meanings or judgments of relative value. Art works differently. A sky, for example, cannot meaningfully be said to have a meaning: there is no semiotics of clouds, and the distinctions between them that delighted Constable are interesting, and of practical use to hill walkers and meteorologists. But though we may say that we like one kind of sky rather than another, it makes no sense to say that one sky is *better* than another. None of these considerations is affected one way or another by the fact that painting more than any thing else has created the modern aesthetics of nature.

The critical discourse provoked by art is of another kind altogether. As I have indicated, it begins in the primitive response that is the *effect* of the object upon the spectator. This effect is itself of a specific and distinctive kind: it is not to be confused with aesthetic responses to other kinds of man-made object such as buildings, streets, canals, cities, textiles, tools, clothes, foodstuffs etc. or with our feelings about natural phenomena such as the plumage of birds, trees, waterfalls or sunsets. Its difference lies in this respect: criticism of a work of art involves the description of its effect, the proposal, or invention, of meanings for it, and the discussion of relative values. It is the task of the artist to create objects or events that have this outcome.

A work of art may, of course, prompt recollections and reminders of such objects, man-made and natural, as I have mentioned. It may also bring to mind, as we say, abstract ideas – such as those codified in geometry, or expressed by such terms as fullness and emptiness, presence and absence –and the abstract properties of material things – such as warmth and coldness, colour and tone, hardness and softness, radiance and darkness. It may provoke thoughts and feelings about order and disorder, pattern and chaos. All or any of these aspects of response, and many others besides, may be compounded in the wordless reaction that is the first thing a work of art demands of the spectator and which is the beginning of its *raison d'être* in the world.

Criticism is the articulation of these complex, or sometimes simple, responses; it uses language to invent and elaborate meanings for the work. The best criticism will be alive to reference and allusion, to ambiguity and nuance, tracing these aspects in the objective elements that constitute the work. But no formulation of critical response, however subtle, is possible without the *specific* provocation of the material actuality of the work. Every such critical formulation is created in the crucible of social discourse: the work has no realisation separable from the language of social intercourse by means of which its meanings are defined. It

is logically impossible for a painting to 'express' the ideas or feelings of its creator: what it 'expresses' is discovered only in the critical conversation that it provokes.

This 'festival' of critical discourse in natural language arises in answer to the historical relations between 'material things' - in this case works of art - that 'are part of the practical reality that surrounds man.' A painting specifically reminds us, through similarities or dissimilarities, of other paintings and other works of art, and prompts thought and discussion as to its place in the purely visual discourse between objects that constitutes the true history of art itself. I mean by this that all art-works refer to other art-works, and are part of a complex process of *material* development. This is the discourse of art itself, the complex 'conversation' that takes place *in art* between artists across time and space. Both terms – 'discourse' and 'conversation' – are intended here as metaphorical. This process has nothing to do with that weary and imprecise art historical notion of 'influence': a much over-used term that serves to obscure distinctions whilst pretending to explain similarities.

The discourse of art is the process of interchange, reaction and interaction that creates the conventions – of subject matter and style – within which the individual talent takes its place within the tradition. It is conducted in the material actions and actualities of art itself. I am speaking of a polyphony of multifarious voices, of artists and critical spectators speaking to others in a community of shared thought and feeling that transcends the limitations of space and time. This is what Bakhtin called the 'dialogic universe': an interactive creative process that is un-fixed, unending and definitively unfinished. The dialectics of that continuum are the proper subject of art history.

Such a truly focussed study would find itself opposed to the 'bourgeois scholarship' that 'sets ideological meaning, abstracted from concrete material, against the individual consciousness of the creator or perceiver,' and that divorces 'ideas' from their realisations in aesthetic experience and

historical circumstance. One such historical circumstance
is the encounter between the art-work and spectator. The
passage from Bakhtin and Medvedev which I quoted in the
first section of this essay concludes: 'We are most inclined to
imagine ideological creation [the making of art, for example,
and its reception] as some inner process of understanding,
comprehension, and perception, and do not notice that in
fact it unfolds externally, for the eye, the ear, the hand. It
is not within us, but between us.' What is between us has
always an ethical dimension. The painter Patrick Heron
wrote: 'Ethics is the aesthetics of behaviour.'

The idea of beauty as an experience of perceived,
apprehended, and inwardly created coherence, a wordless
comprehension of a multiplicity of relations – sensational,
formal, compositional, circumstantial, factual, eventual,
etc. – reinstates the term as a complex, meaningful and
legitimate component of critical utterance. I intend the word
'comprehension' all its senses: a taking hold of and holding
within, an encompassing, an understanding, a knowing.
Beauty is a way of knowing.

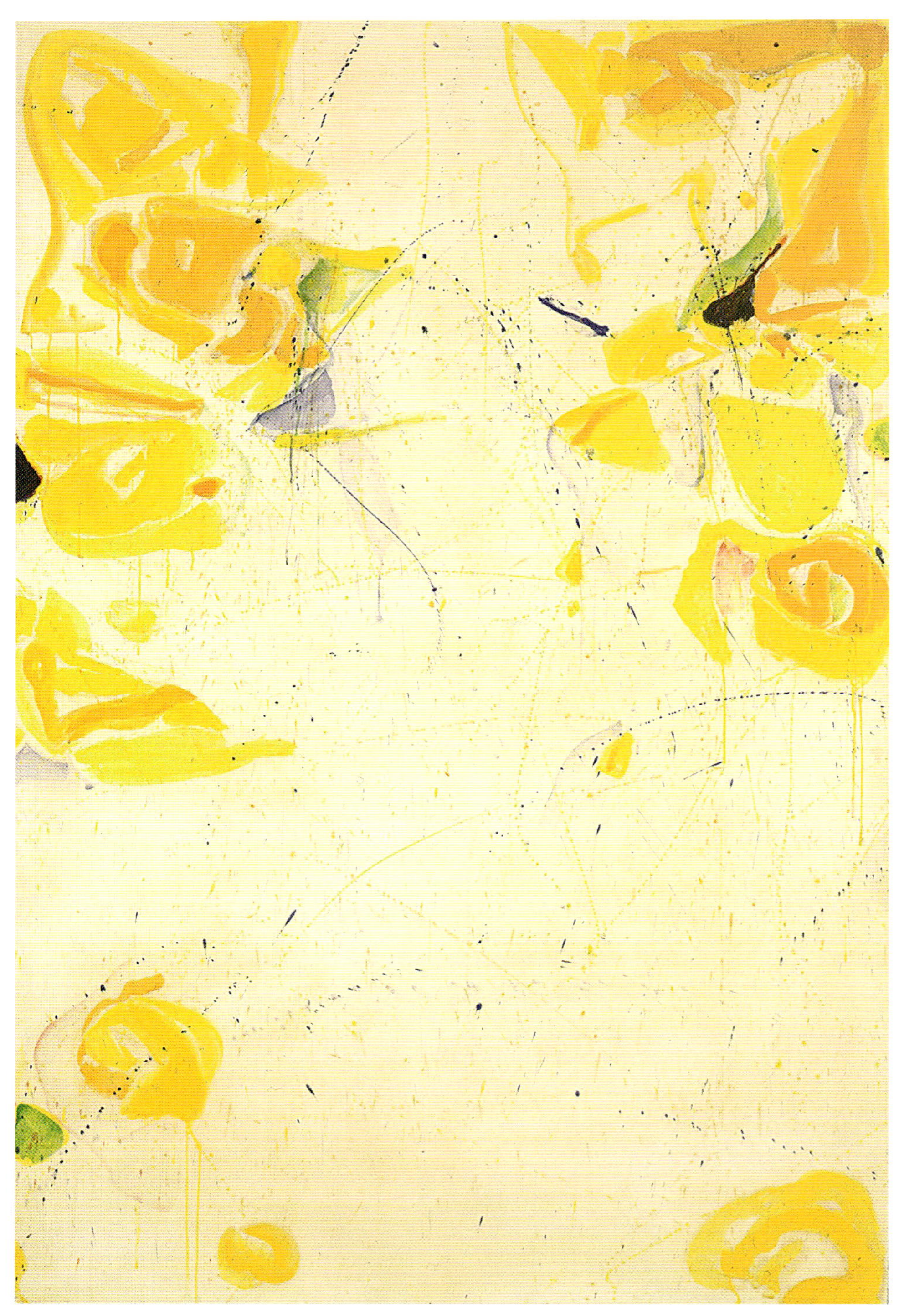

Sam Francis, (1923-1994)
Untitled
1959
Oil on paper mounted on canvas
166 x 111 cms ($65\frac{1}{3}$ x $43\frac{7}{10}$ ins)

Sam Francis: *Untitled* (1959)

What do we make of this tall object, this celebration of
yellow, this emptiness of paper almost encircled by yellow
whorls, whirls and blobs? I remember that in England we
speak of marsh marigolds, *caltha palustris*, as mayblobs, a
singularly down-to-earth name for a spring water flower that
lives up to its proper name, its gold being startling in its
sunny brightness. Certainly one has the sense of a pool, of
a purity stained by floating manifestations of golden yellow,
revolving, bunching, floating free. We look into translucence,
a rectangular pool of light, aquatic, aerial, atmospheric.
Elemental! Empty.

This reverie may seem fanciful. Of course: because it is
in the nature of reverie to be so. We are contemplating a
painting that invites fantasia, an object that invites reflection
on the yellowness of things yellow, the yellows of yellowness.
Yellow: the colour of marsh marigolds, sunflowers and
buttercups, lemons and bananas, Easter chicks and toy
ducks. But above all, for Matisse, it is the colour-sign for
that origin of pure light, the sun.

For *Untitled* (1959) is nothing more, or less, than a
brilliant evocation of our diurnal element, light: it is a
celebration of sunlight, a reminder of the most ancient and
persistent festivals. Looking into this painting we are looking
into infinity; its yellows expand: they occupy the eye, they
create a sensation of all-over yellowness. In fact, they are
peripheral to the total composition; they give their light, by
an optical effect, to an empty expanse of plain paper. Those
random, seemingly accidental splashes and spatterings of
black and blue ink remind us that this is a material thing
in our immediate space, in our circumstantial world. That
empty immensity is the sign for infinity.

References

Quotations from Matisse are from various texts in *Matisse on Art*, edited by Jack D. Flam (London 1973). Gaston Bachelard's remarks on 'intimate immensity' are from Chap. 8 of The *Poetics of Space* translated by Maria Jolis (Boston 1969). Matisse: 'Here is a country where light plays the leading role…' Flam p.114. *The Relevance of the Beautiful and Other Essays* by Hans-Georg Gadamer, translated by Nicholas Walter, is published by Cambridge University Press (Cambridge 1986). Susan Sontag's 'An Argument About Beauty' is from *At the Same Time* (London 2007). M.M.Bakhtin and P.N. Medvedev are quoted from *The Formal Method of Literary Scholarship* (Baltimore and London 1978). Tobey is quoted in the catalogue to an exhibition at Galerie Beyeler, Basel, in December 1970 – February 1971. 'Ethics and aesthetics are one': proposition 6.421 Ludwig Wittgenstein, *Tractatus Logico-Philosophicus* (London 1922). Wallace Stevens's writes of resemblance in the first of 'Three Academic Pieces' in *The Necessary Angel* (London 1960). Alberto Giacometti is quoted from an interview with Pierre Schneider 'At the Louvre' in Encounter, March, 1966. text 'The Creative Act' is included in *Marchand du Sel: écrits de Marcel Duchamp* ed. by Michel Sanouillet (Paris 1958) Maurice Merleau-Ponty's 'Eye and Mind' 1961 is in *The Merleau-Ponty Aesthetics Reader* ed. Galen A. Johnson (Evanston, Illinois 1993) Suzanne K. Langer is quoted from 'Artistic Perception and "Natural Light"' in *Problems of Art* (London 1957). Matisse wrote about 'composition' in 'Notes of a Painter' 1908 (Flam p. 35) Stephen Dedalus talks of Aquinian aesthetics in *A Portrait of the Artist as a Young Man* (chapter 5) by James Joyce (1916). Patrick Heron is quoted from 'Submerged Rhythm' in *The Changing Forms of Art* (London 1955)

Catalogue

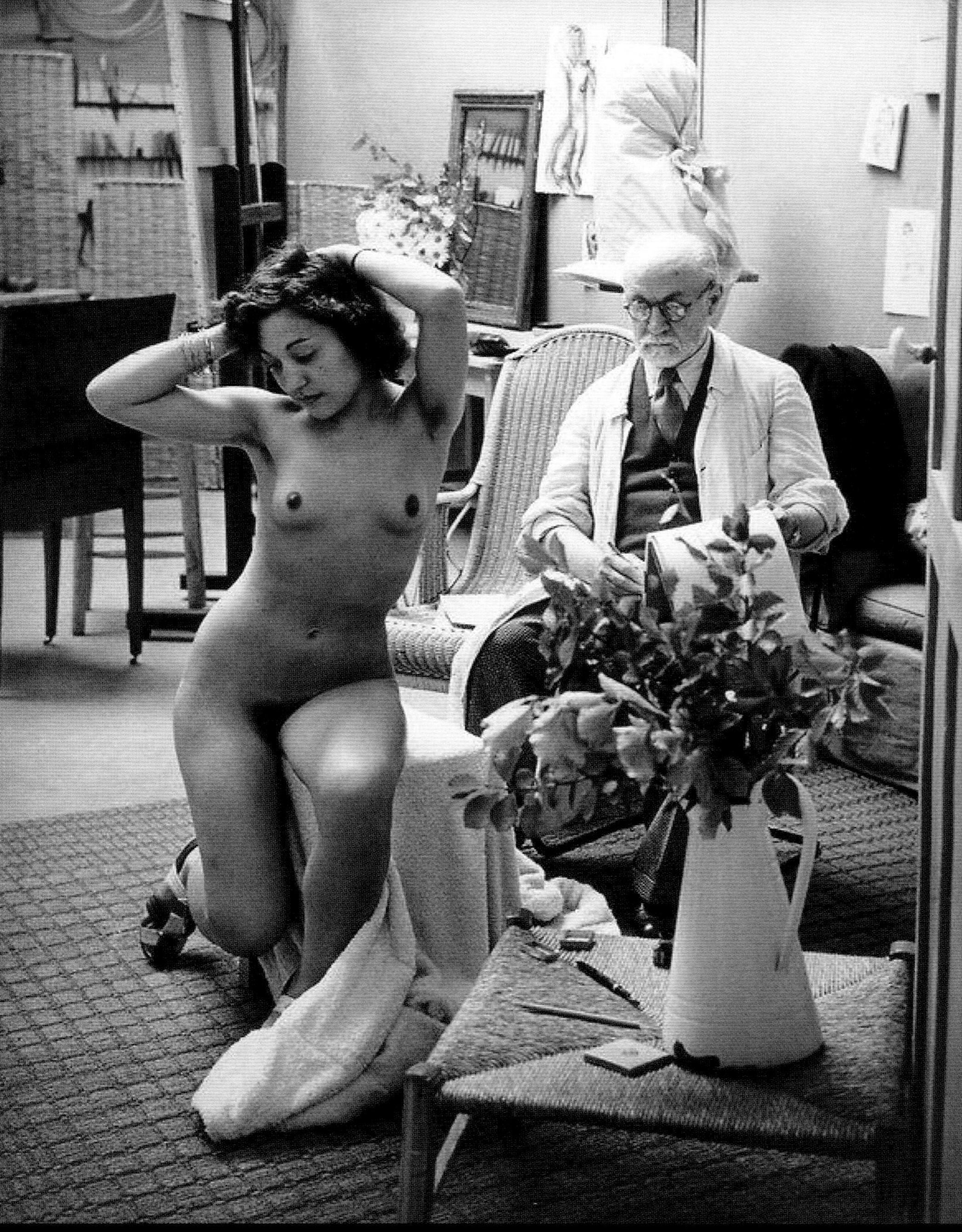

Henri Matisse drawing in his studio, 1939, Brassai

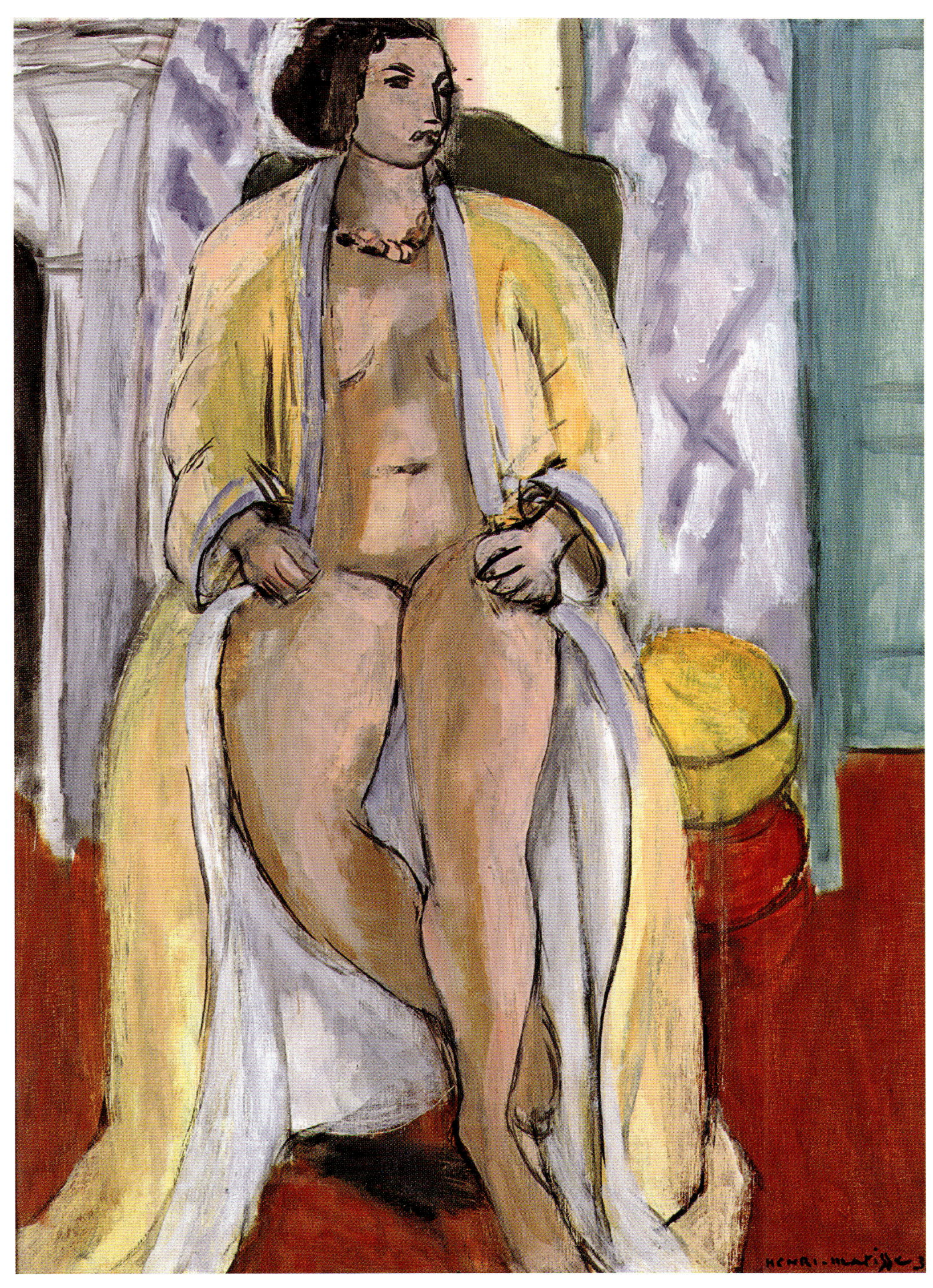

Henri Matisse
Nu au peignoir
1933
Oil on canvas
65 x 46 cms (25½ x 18 ins)

Henri Matisse
Jeune femme assise en robe grise
1942
Oil on canvas
46.3 x 38.2 cm (18¼ x 15 ins)

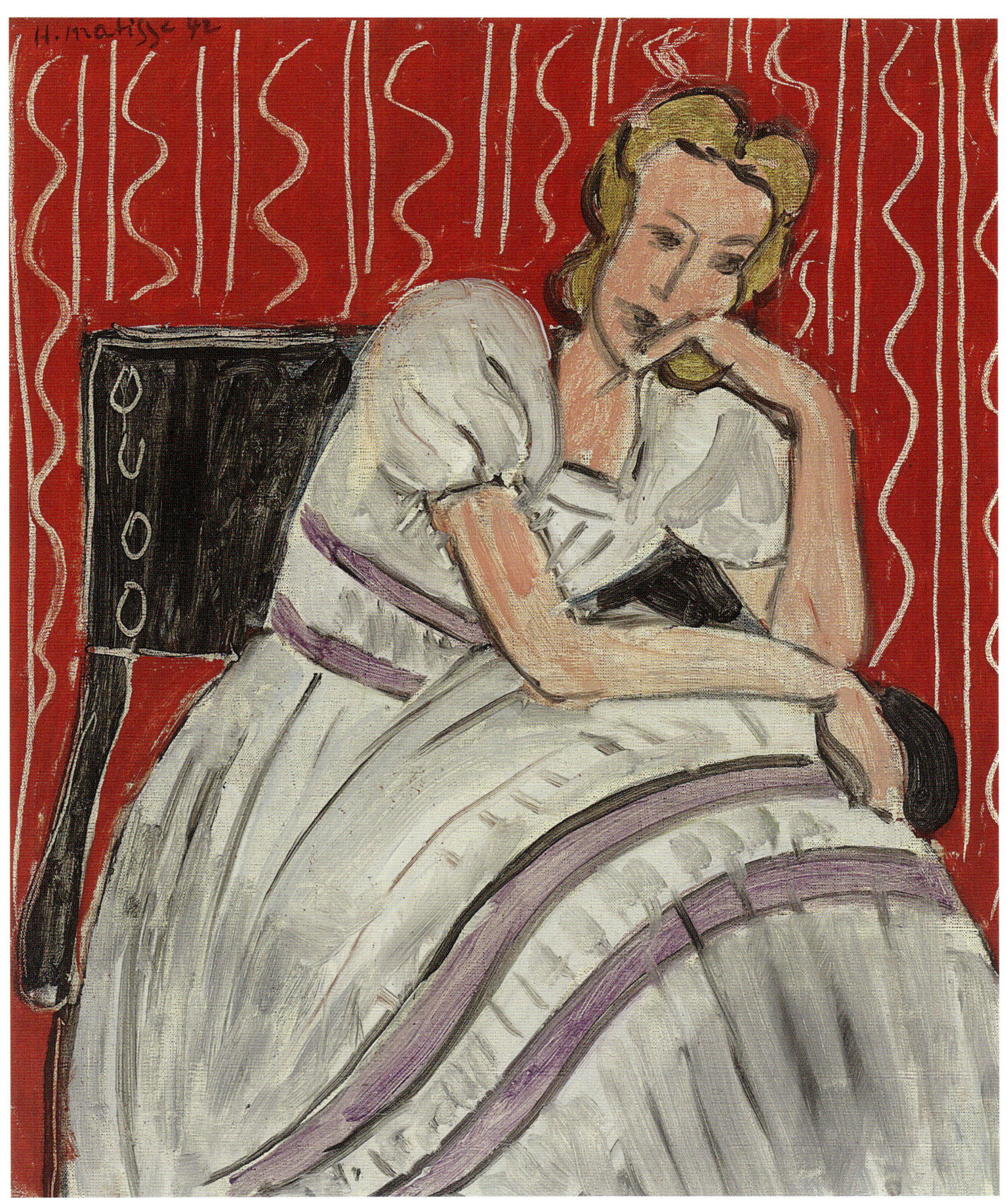

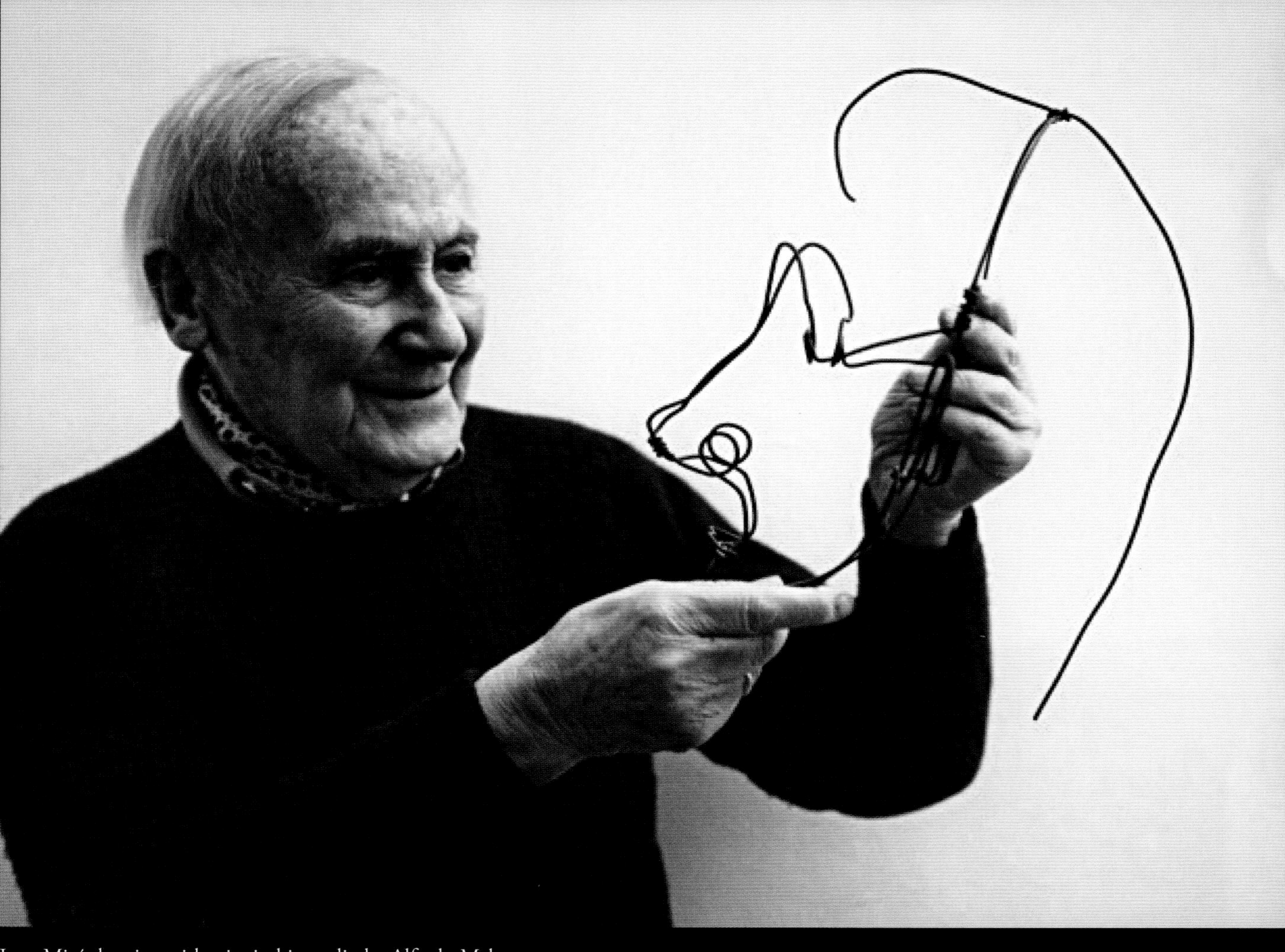

Joan Miró drawing with wire in his studio by Alfredo Melgar

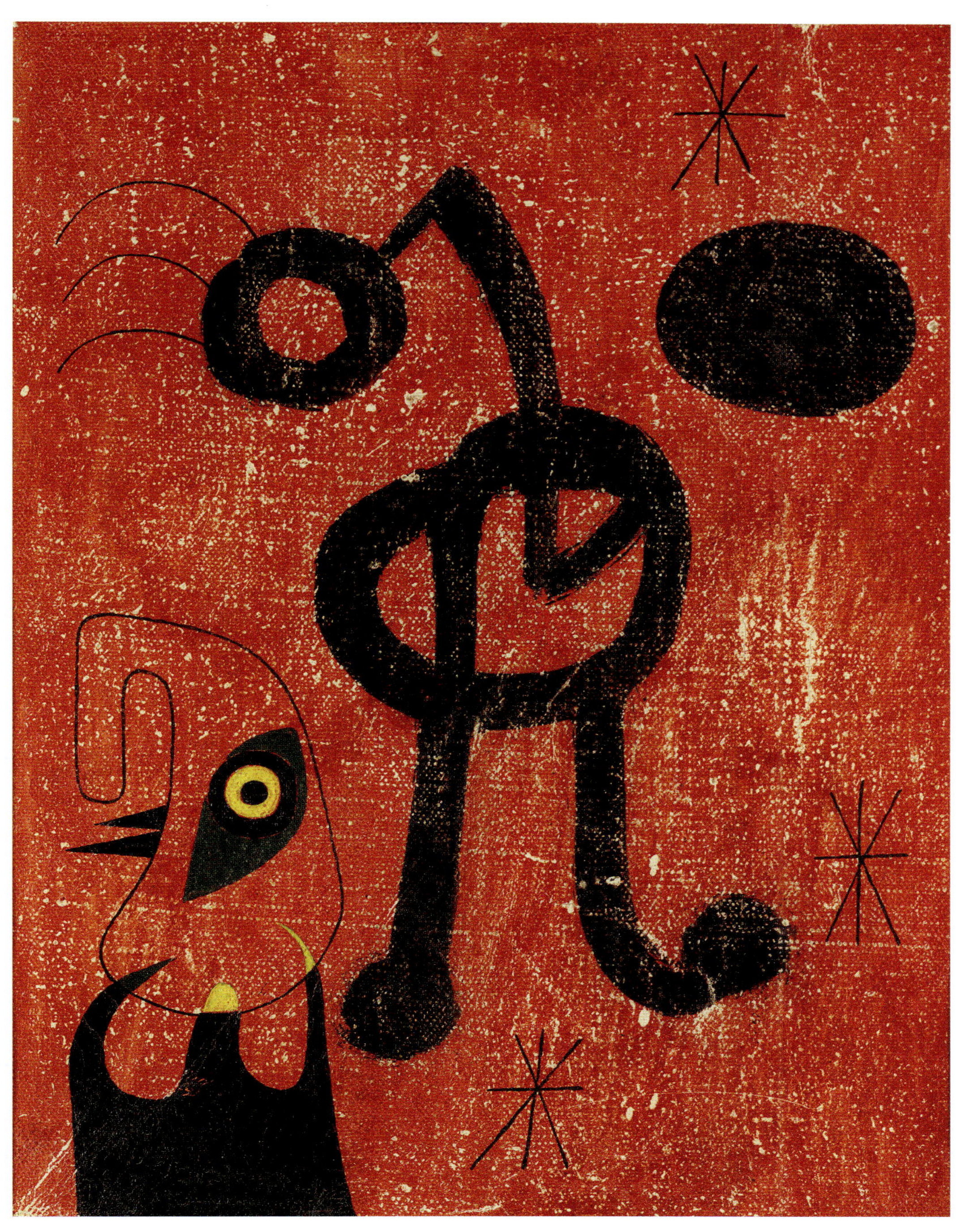

Joan Miró
Femme et oiseau devant le soleil
1944
Oil on canvas
34.9 x 26.7 cms (13¾ x 10½ ins)

Joan Miró
Femme et oiseau devant la nuit
1944
Oil on canvas
35.2 x 27 cms (13⅞ x 10⅝ ins)

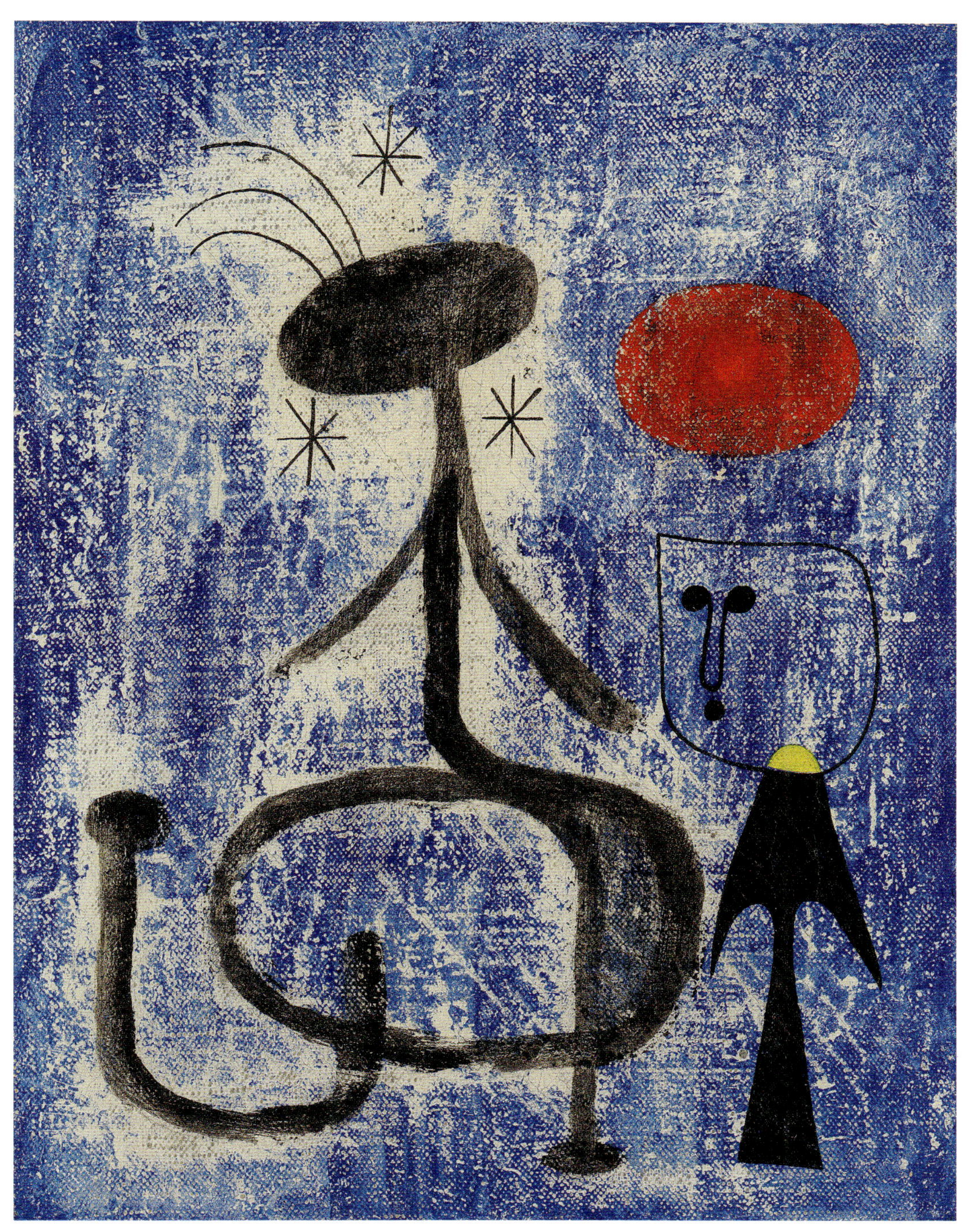

Joan Miró
Femmes devant la lune
1944
Oil and pastel on canvas
26 x 35 cms (10¼ x 13¾ ins)

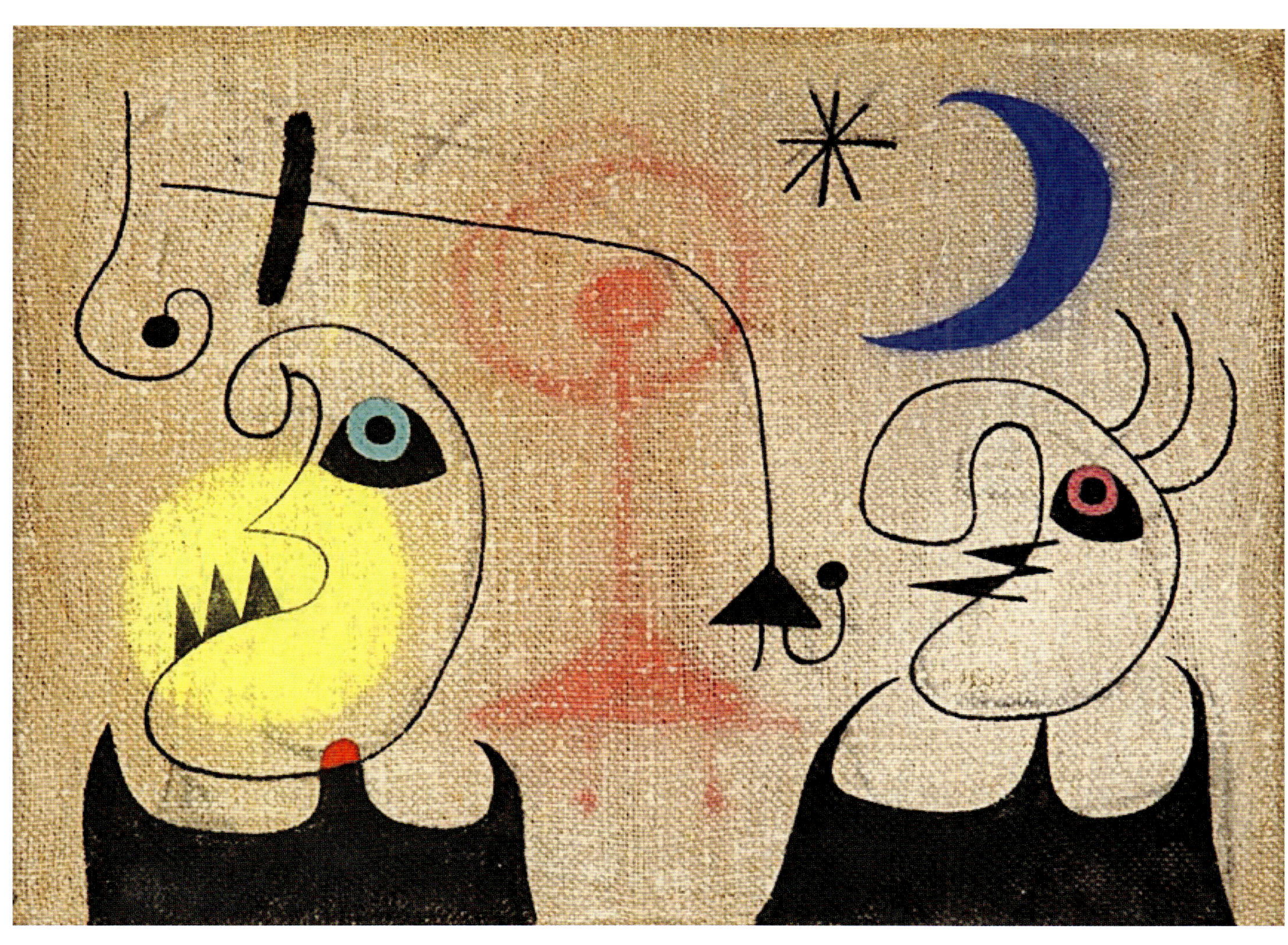

Joan Miró
Paysage
1974
Oil on canvas
130 x 97 cms (51⅛ x 38¼ ins)

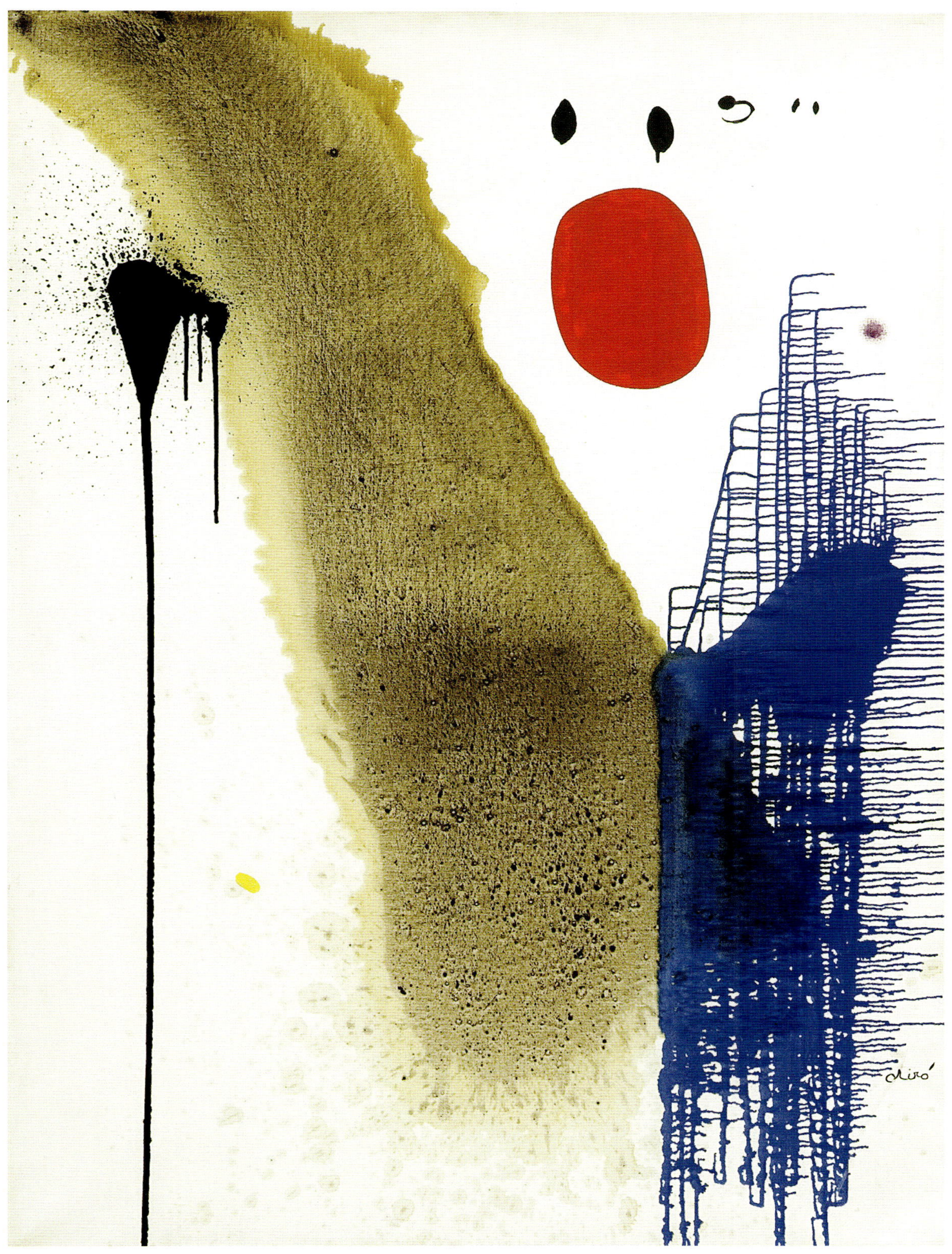

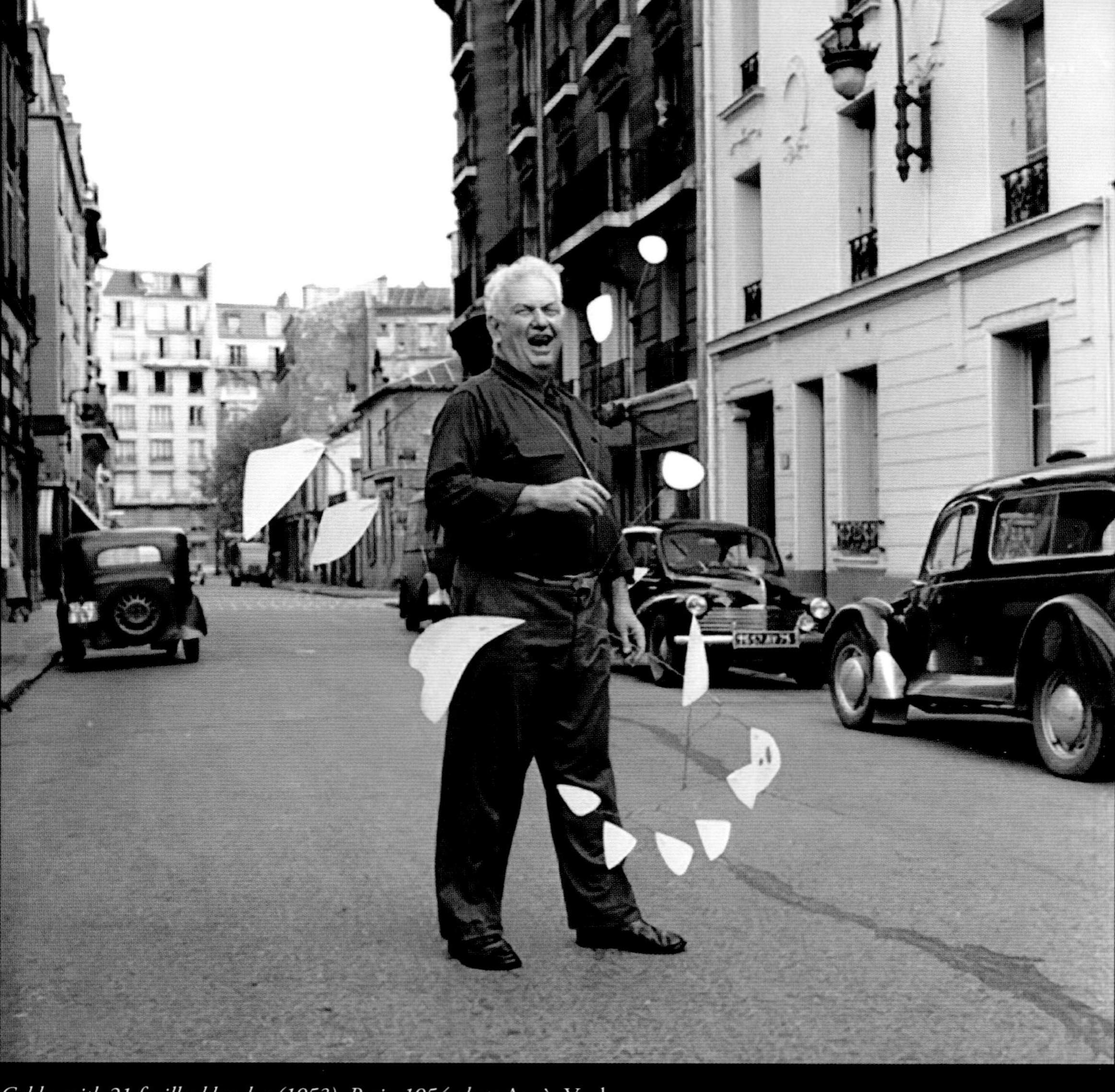

Calder with 21 feuilles blanches (1953), Paris, 1954 photo Agnès Varda

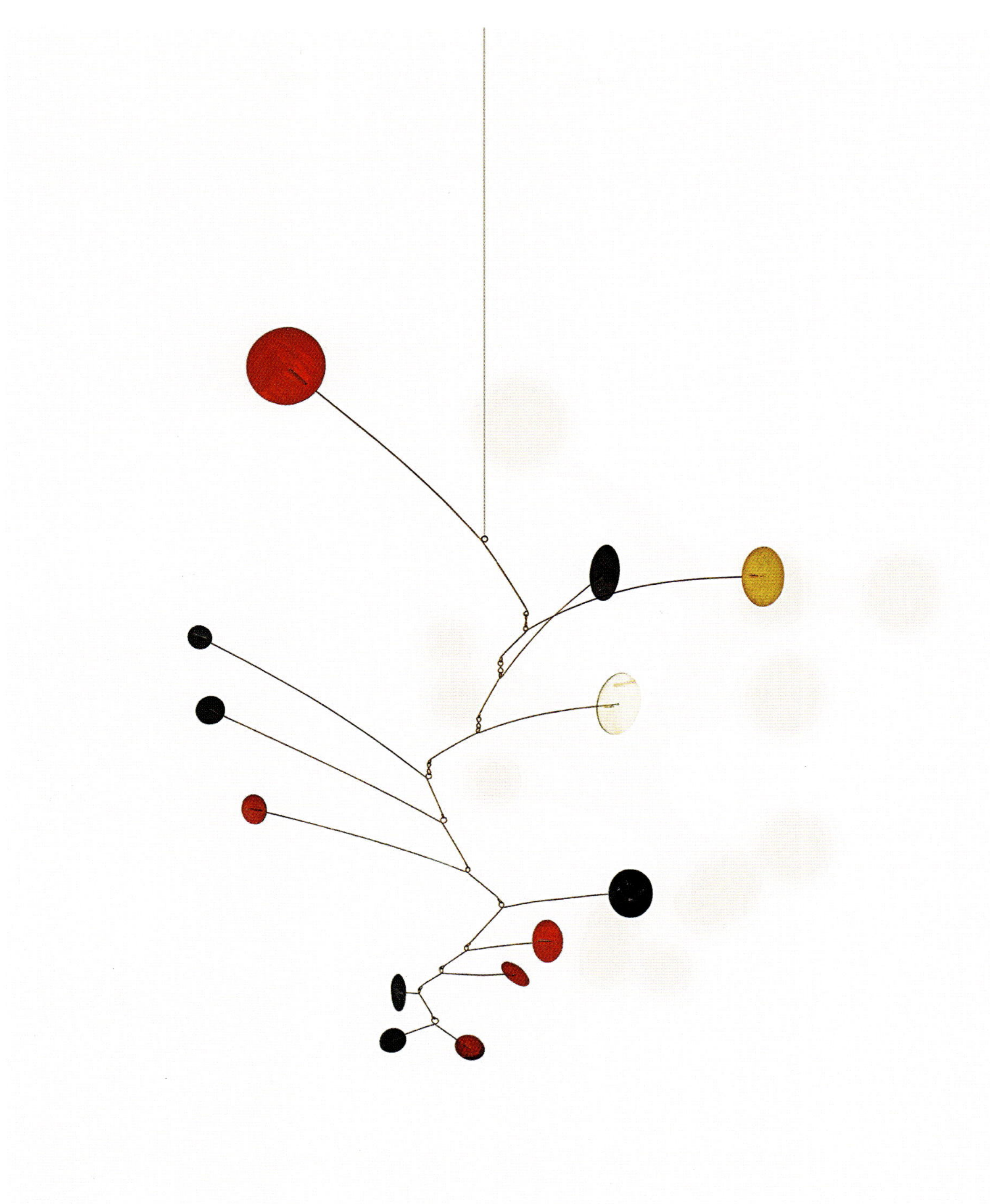

Alexander Calder
Sans Titre
1947
Hanging mobile: painted sheet metal and wire
86 x 71 cms (33.86 x 27.95 ins)

Alexander Calder
Petit Mobile sur Pied
1953
Standing mobile - painted sheet metal, rod and wire
66.7 x 50.8 x 43.2 cms

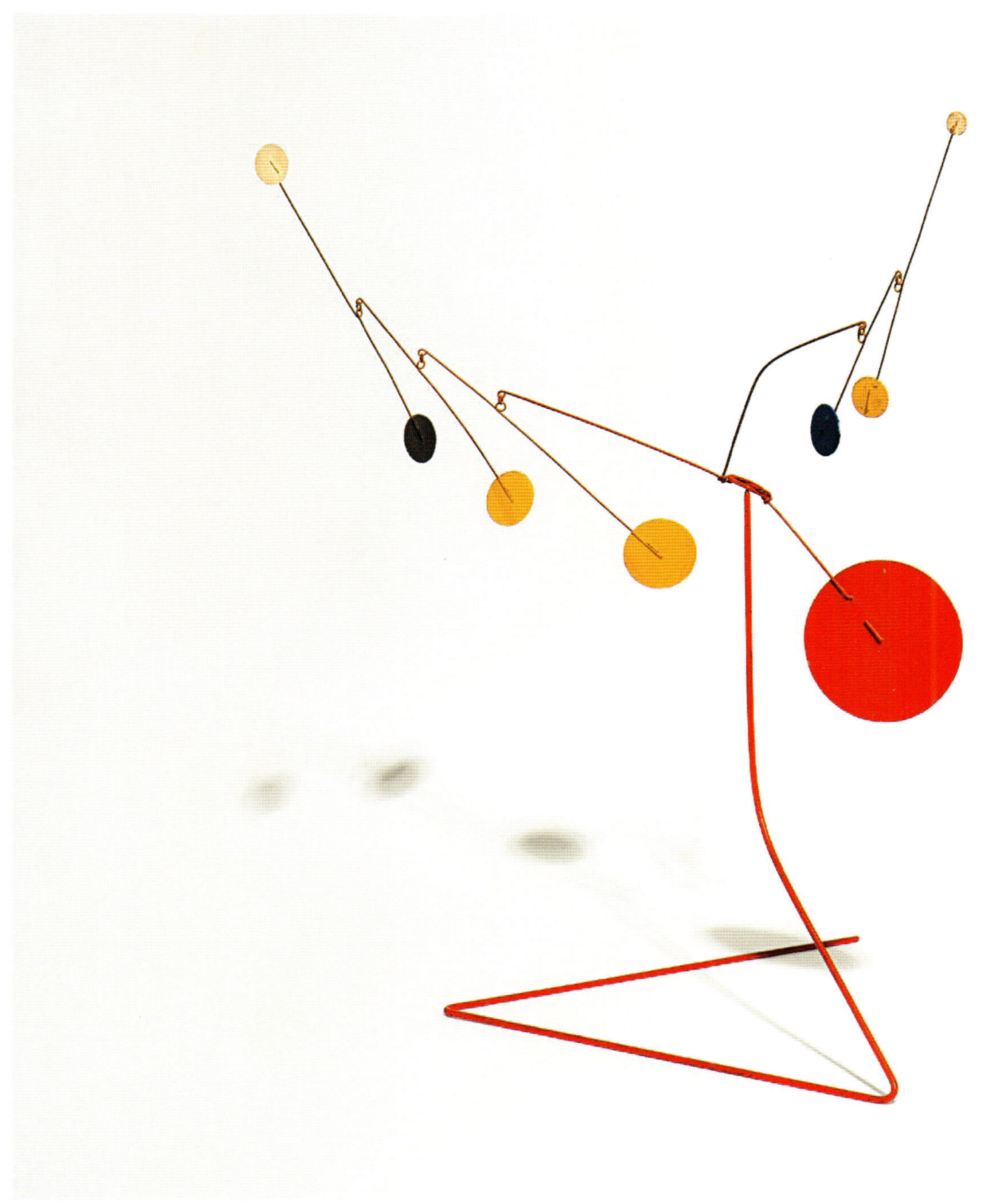

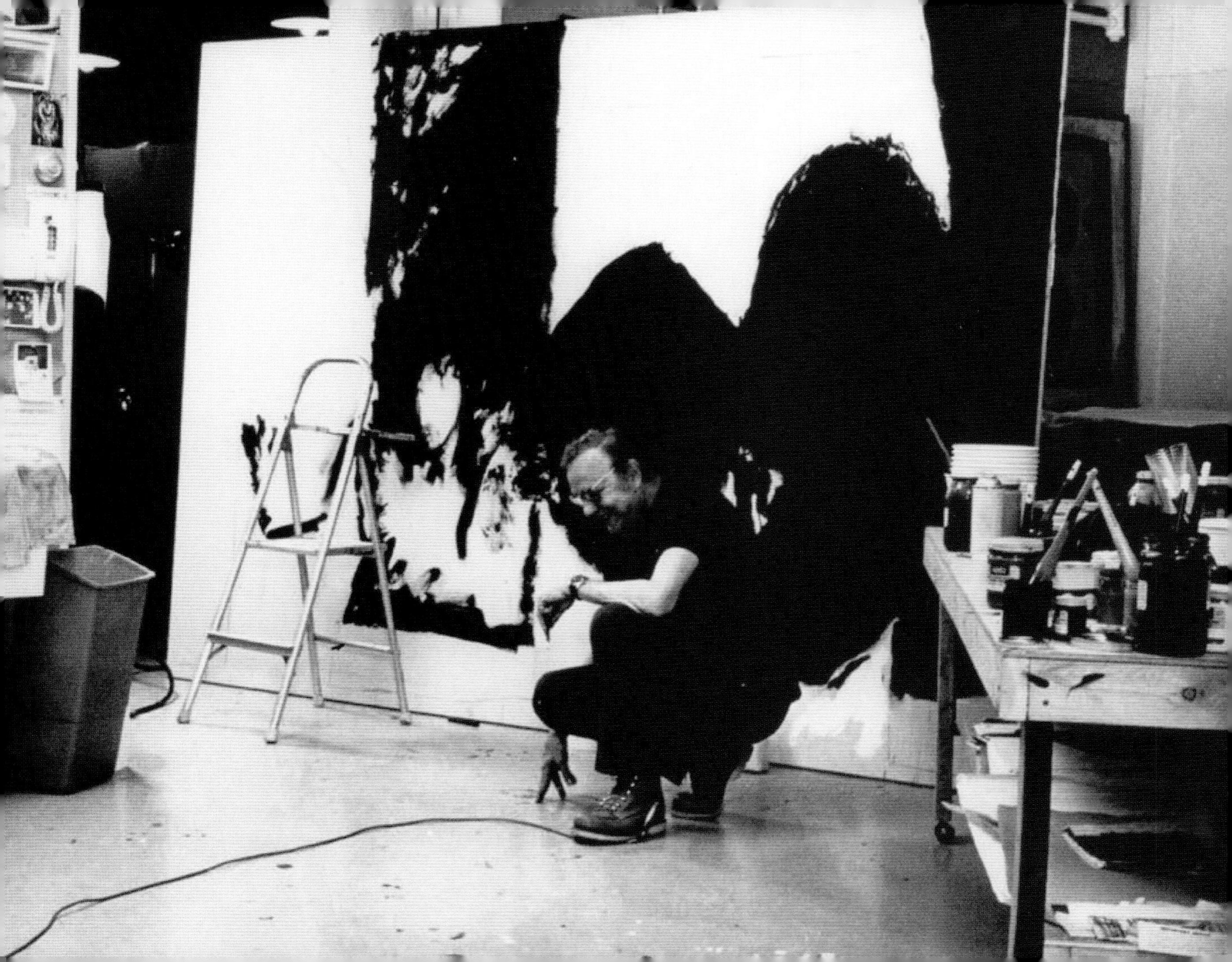

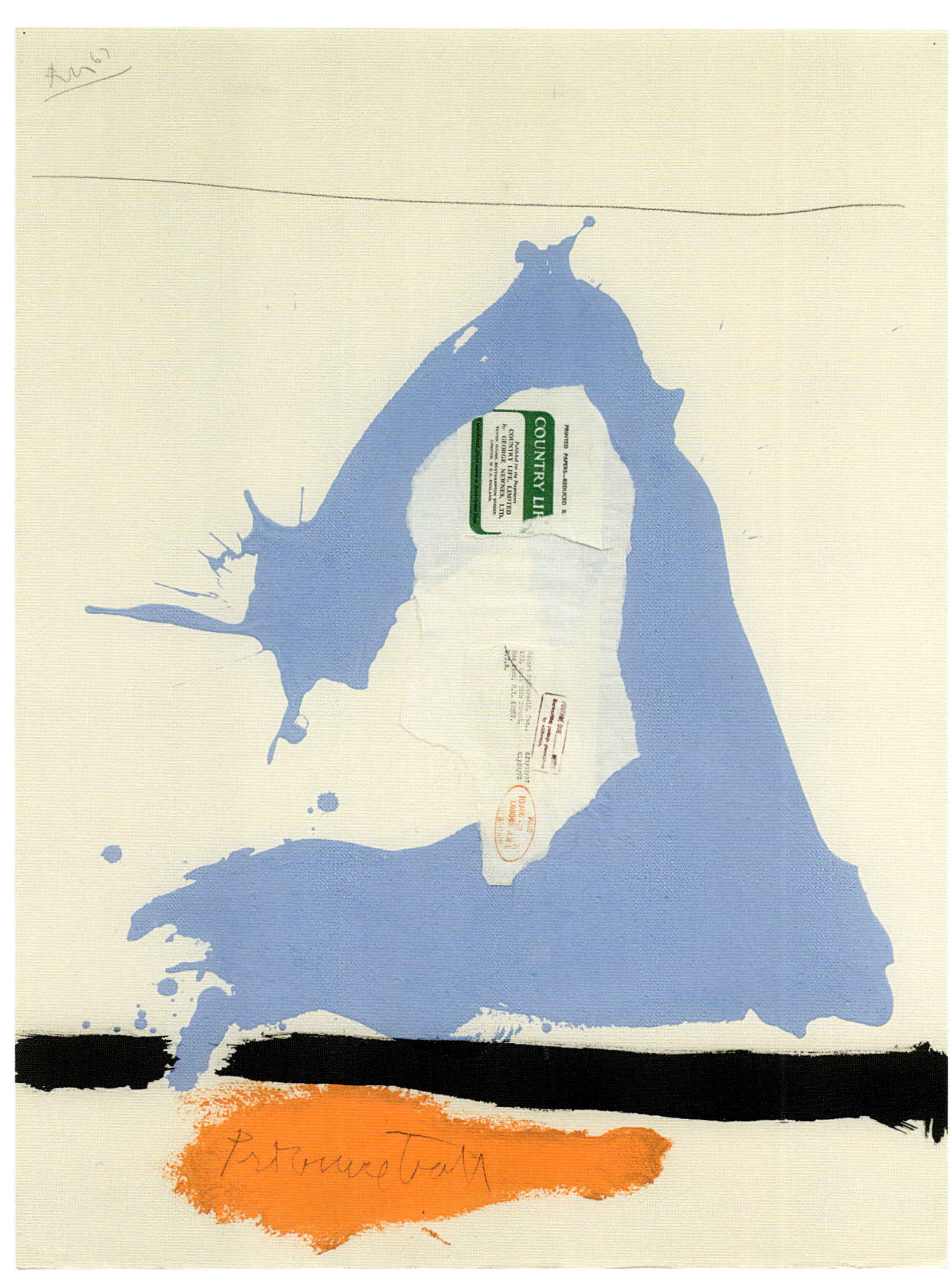

Robert Motherwell
Country Life
1967
Acrylic, graphite and paper collage on paper
77.5 x 56.5 cms (30½ x 22¼ ins)

Robert Motherwell
Torino
1975-1976
(Alternative Title: *Torino Collage*), 1975-76
Acrylic and pasted papers on canvas mounted on Masonite
121.9 x 91.4 cms (48 x 36 ins)

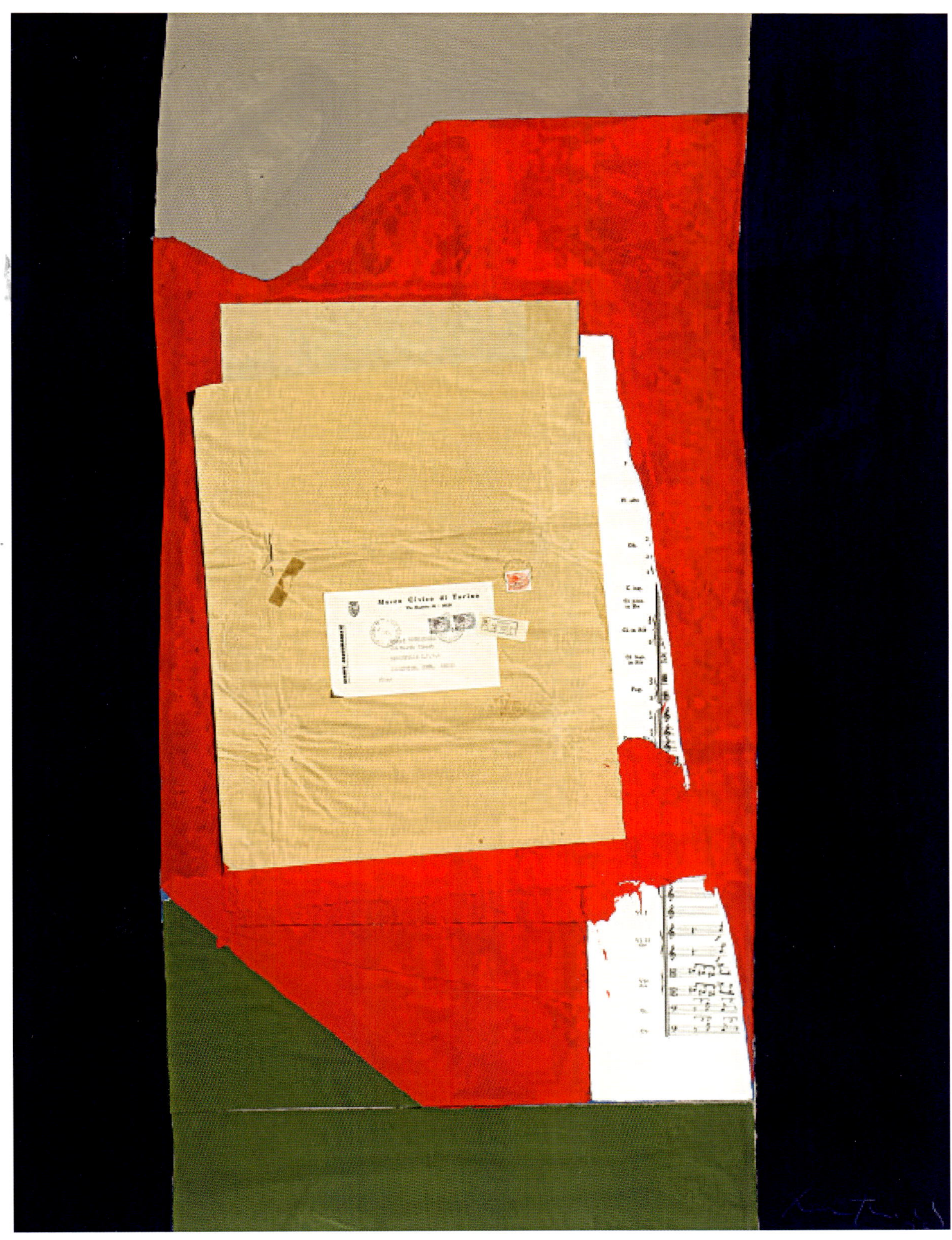

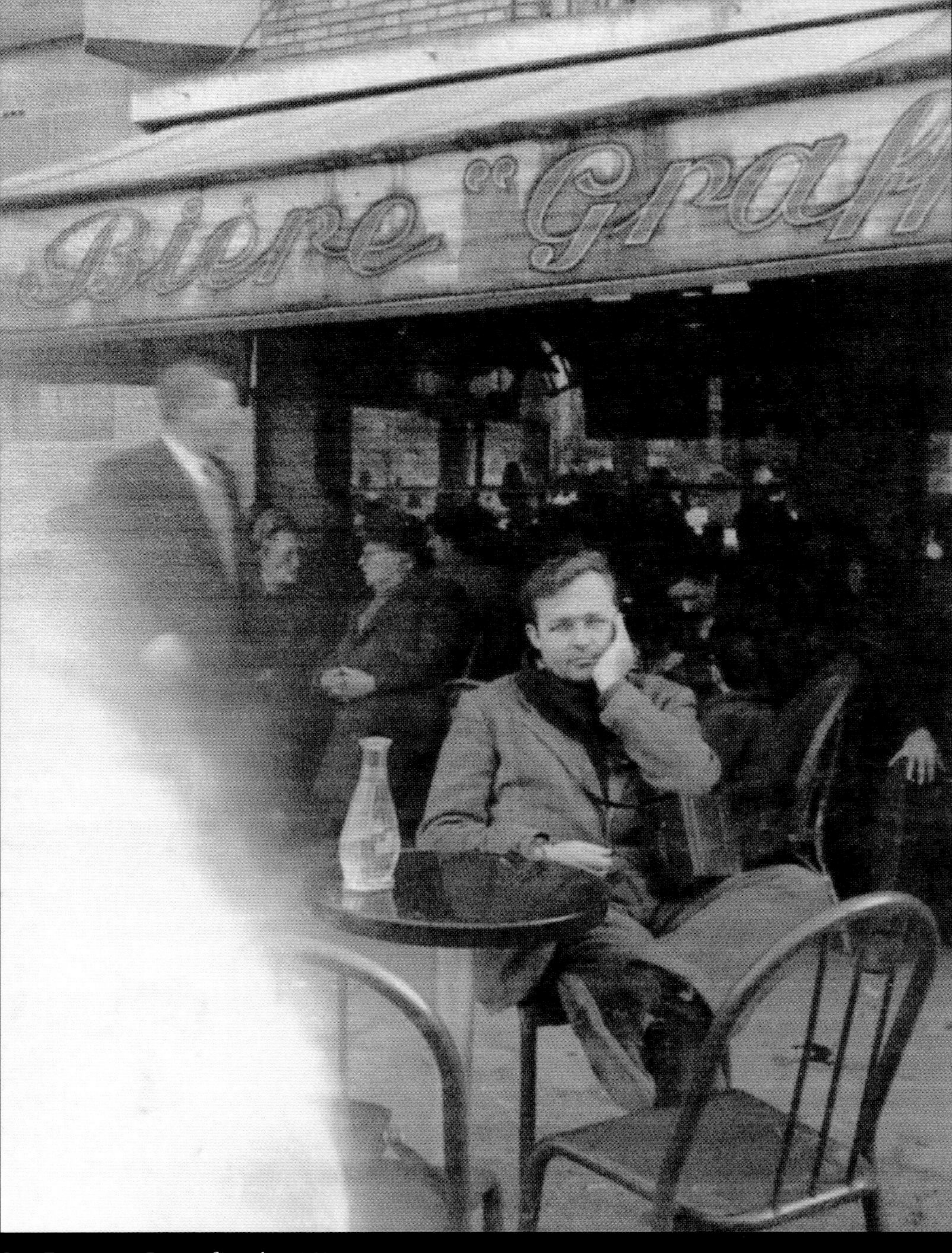

Sam Francis at a Paris café in the 1950s

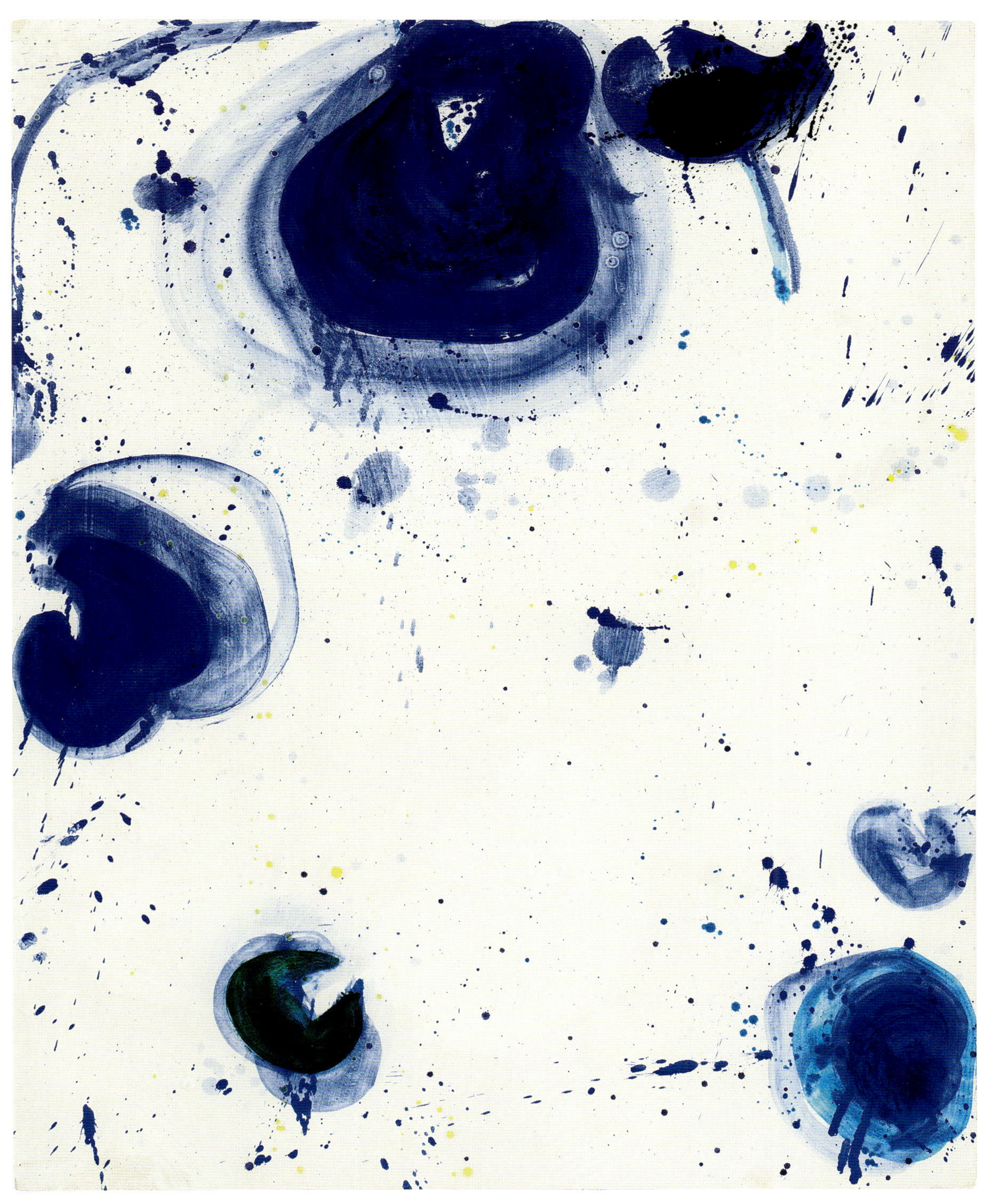

Sam Francis (1923-1994)
Blue Balls series [Alternate Title: Blue Balls] (SF60-1000)
1960
Oil on paper (painted in Paris)
55.9 x 44.7 cms (22 x 17⅝ ins)

Sam Francis
E V
1970-71
Acrylic on canvas
304.8 x 182.9 cms (120 x 72 ins)

Published on the occasion of the exhibition Bonheur de Vivre
18th March - 31st May 2016 at
Bernard Jacobson Gallery
28 Duke Street St. James's
020 7734 3431
mail@jacobsongallery.com
www.jacobsongallery.com

British Cataloguing-in-Publication Data
A catalogue record for this book is available
From the British Library

ISBN: 978-187-278-4571

Coordinated by Robert Delaney
Designed and printed by C A Design, Hong Kong